Agile Methodologies
A Comprehensive Guide to Agile Practices and Principles

May Sherry

Table of Content

Introduction

- **The Agile Revolution:** Overview of Agile's emergence and its impact on software development.
- **Why Agile Matters:** Benefits of Agile methodologies and their relevance in modern projects.

Chapter 1: Understanding Agile

- **What is Agile?:** Definition and key principles of Agile.
- **The Agile Manifesto:** Core values and principles.
- **Agile vs. Traditional Methodologies:** Comparison with Waterfall and other traditional methods.

Chapter 2: Agile Frameworks and Methodologies

- **Scrum:**
    - Overview of Scrum.
    - Roles (Scrum Master, Product Owner, Development Team).
    - Artifacts (Product Backlog, Sprint Backlog, Increment).
    - Events (Sprint, Sprint Planning, Daily Scrum, Sprint Review, Sprint Retrospective).
- **Kanban:**
    - Principles of Kanban.
    - Kanban Boards and Workflow Visualization.
    - WIP Limits and Continuous Delivery.
- **Extreme Programming (XP):**
    - Core Practices (Pair Programming, Test-Driven Development, Continuous Integration).
    - Benefits and Challenges of XP.
- **Lean:**
    - Lean Principles.
    - Value Stream Mapping and Waste Reduction.
    - Lean and Agile Integration.
- **Other Frameworks:** Overview of additional frameworks like Crystal, DSDM, and FDD.

Chapter 3: Implementing Agile

- **Getting Started with Agile:** Steps to initiate an Agile transformation.
- **Building an Agile Team:** Roles, responsibilities, and team dynamics.

- **Agile Planning and Estimation:** Techniques for planning sprints, user stories, and estimating work.
- **Managing Backlogs:** Creating and maintaining Product and Sprint Backlogs.

Chapter 4: Agile Practices

- **Daily Standups:** Purpose and best practices.
- **Sprint Reviews and Retrospectives:** How to conduct effective reviews and retrospectives.
- **Continuous Integration and Continuous Delivery:** Key concepts and practices.
- **Test-Driven Development (TDD):** Principles and benefits.

Chapter 5: Agile Tools and Technologies

- **JIRA:** Features and how to use it for Agile management.
- **Trello and Kanban Tools:** Setting up Kanban boards.
- **Version Control Systems (e.g., Git):** Integration with Agile practices.
- **Collaboration Tools:** Slack, Confluence, and other communication tools.

Chapter 6: Scaling Agile

- **Scaling Frameworks:** Overview of SAFe, LeSS, and Spotify Model.
- **Challenges in Scaling Agile:** Common issues and solutions.
- **Case Studies:** Examples of organizations that successfully scaled Agile.

Chapter 7: Measuring Agile Success

- **Key Performance Indicators (KPIs):** Metrics for Agile success.
- **Feedback Loops:** How to gather and utilize feedback.
- **Continuous Improvement:** Techniques for ongoing enhancement.

Chapter 8: Agile and Organizational Culture

- **Creating an Agile Culture:** Principles for fostering an Agile mindset.
- **Leadership in Agile:** Role of leaders in Agile transformations.
- **Training and Coaching:** Importance of training and the role of Agile coaches.

Chapter 9: Future of Agile

- **Emerging Trends:** Latest trends and innovations in Agile.

- **Agile in Non-Software Environments:** Applications of Agile outside software development.
- **The Evolution of Agile Practices:** How Agile is evolving and adapting to new challenges.

Conclusion

- **Moving Forward:** Guidance on implementing and evolving Agile practices in your organization.

Introduction

The Agile Revolution: Overview of Agile's emergence and its impact on software development.

The Agile Revolution represents a paradigm shift in software development, transforming traditional project management and development practices. Emerging in the early 2000s, Agile was born out of a desire to overcome the limitations of the Waterfall model, which often struggled with rigidity and delayed feedback. The Agile Manifesto, published in 2001 by a group of software developers, laid the groundwork for this revolution. It emphasized iterative development, customer collaboration, and responsiveness to change, challenging the conventional methods that relied heavily on upfront planning and sequential phases.

The impact of Agile on software development has been profound and multifaceted. Agile methodologies, such as Scrum, Kanban, and Extreme Programming (XP), introduced a more flexible and iterative approach to development. These methodologies prioritize continuous delivery, allowing teams to release incremental updates and gather user feedback more frequently. This iterative process not only accelerates the development cycle but also ensures that the product evolves in alignment with user needs and market demands. Agile practices foster greater collaboration among team members and stakeholders, enhancing communication and transparency throughout the project lifecycle.

The Agile Revolution has also influenced broader aspects of organizational culture and project management. By emphasizing adaptability and iterative progress, Agile has encouraged a shift towards more collaborative and cross-functional teams. This cultural shift promotes a proactive approach to problem-solving and encourages ongoing improvements, leading to higher-quality software and more satisfied customers. Additionally, Agile has spurred the adoption of complementary practices, such as DevOps and Continuous Integration/Continuous Deployment (CI/CD), further enhancing the efficiency and effectiveness of software development processes.

The Agile Revolution has redefined the landscape of software development, moving away from rigid, linear methodologies toward a more dynamic and responsive approach. Its emphasis on flexibility, collaboration, and iterative progress has reshaped how software is developed, delivered, and maintained, setting new standards for quality and customer satisfaction in the industry.

Why Agile Matters: Benefits of Agile methodologies and their relevance in modern projects.

Agile methodologies have become integral to modern project management due to their ability to deliver value and adaptability in today's fast-paced environment. One of the primary benefits of Agile is its emphasis on iterative development, which allows teams to produce incremental updates and continuously refine the product based on real-time feedback. This iterative process reduces the risk of large-scale project failures by ensuring that any issues or misalignments are identified and addressed early in the development cycle. By prioritizing regular feedback and adaptability, Agile methodologies help teams stay aligned with changing market demands and customer needs, ultimately leading to a more relevant and effective end product.

Another significant advantage of Agile is its focus on collaboration and communication. Agile practices, such as daily stand-ups and sprint reviews, foster a culture of transparency and teamwork. These regular touchpoints help ensure that all team members and stakeholders are on the same page, promoting a shared understanding of goals and progress. This collaborative environment enhances problem-solving and decision-making, as issues can be addressed quickly and efficiently through collective input. The emphasis on stakeholder involvement also ensures that the final product better aligns with user expectations and delivers greater value.

Agile methodologies also contribute to increased efficiency and productivity. By breaking projects into smaller, manageable tasks, Agile allows teams to focus on delivering functional components in short cycles. This approach not only accelerates the development process but also enables teams to prioritize tasks based on business value and urgency. Agile's flexibility in adjusting priorities and scope helps optimize resource allocation and minimizes waste, leading to more efficient project execution.

In modern projects, the relevance of Agile methodologies is further underscored by the rapid pace of technological change and the need for organizations to remain competitive. Agile's ability to adapt to evolving requirements and its focus on delivering continuous value make it particularly well-suited for industries where innovation and responsiveness are critical. By fostering a culture of continuous improvement and embracing change, Agile methodologies help organizations stay ahead of the curve and achieve their strategic objectives in a dynamic and challenging landscape.

Chapter 1: Understanding Agile

What is Agile?: Definition and key principles of Agile.

Agile is a project management and software development methodology that emphasizes flexibility, collaboration, and iterative progress. At its core, Agile is defined by a set of principles and practices that prioritize delivering value through incremental development and continuous feedback. Unlike traditional methodologies that follow a linear, sequential approach, Agile promotes an adaptive process where requirements and solutions evolve through the collaborative efforts of cross-functional teams.

The foundation of Agile is articulated in the Agile Manifesto, which outlines four key values and twelve principles. The core values of Agile emphasize:

1. **Individuals and Interactions Over Processes and Tools:** Agile prioritizes effective communication and collaboration among team members and stakeholders over rigid adherence to processes and tools.
2. **Working Software Over Comprehensive Documentation:** Agile focuses on delivering functional software that meets user needs rather than extensive documentation. This approach encourages practical, actionable results.
3. **Customer Collaboration Over Contract Negotiation:** Agile encourages ongoing collaboration with customers and stakeholders throughout the project to ensure that the end product aligns with their evolving needs and expectations.
4. **Responding to Change Over Following a Plan:** Agile values adaptability and responsiveness to change, recognizing that project requirements may shift as new information and insights emerge.

The twelve principles of Agile further elaborate on these values, providing guidance on how to implement them in practice. These principles include delivering working software frequently, welcoming changing requirements, maintaining a sustainable pace of work, and fostering a collaborative environment where teams are empowered to make decisions. Agile methodologies, such as Scrum, Kanban, and Extreme Programming (XP), operationalize these principles through specific practices and frameworks, each tailored to support iterative development, continuous improvement, and customer-focused outcomes.

Agile represents a shift towards a more flexible and responsive approach to project management and development. By emphasizing collaboration, adaptability, and iterative progress, Agile methodologies help teams deliver high-quality products that meet user needs while navigating the complexities of modern project environments.

The Agile Manifesto: Core values and principles.

The Agile Manifesto, crafted in 2001 by a group of software developers, serves as the cornerstone of Agile methodologies, encapsulating a revolutionary approach to project management and software development. At its heart, the Manifesto is built on four core values and twelve guiding principles that collectively define the Agile philosophy and its emphasis on flexibility, collaboration, and customer satisfaction.

The four core values of the Agile Manifesto are:

1. **Individuals and Interactions Over Processes and Tools:** Agile places higher importance on the effectiveness of team communication and collaboration rather than the strict adherence to processes and tools. It recognizes that a well-functioning team with open dialogue is more crucial to project success than rigid procedures or technological constraints.
2. **Working Software Over Comprehensive Documentation:** The emphasis is on delivering functional software that meets user needs rather than producing extensive documentation. While documentation is still important, Agile prioritizes tangible outcomes and user-centric results over detailed paperwork.
3. **Customer Collaboration Over Contract Negotiation:** Agile encourages ongoing engagement with customers and stakeholders throughout the development process. This continuous interaction ensures that the product aligns with evolving customer needs and expectations, rather than rigidly adhering to pre-defined contractual terms.
4. **Responding to Change Over Following a Plan:** Agile values the ability to adapt to changing requirements and conditions over sticking to a fixed plan. This flexibility allows teams to incorporate new insights and respond to emerging needs, ensuring that the product remains relevant and effective.

The twelve principles of the Agile Manifesto elaborate on these values, providing practical guidance for implementing Agile practices. They advocate for delivering working software frequently, welcoming changing requirements even late in development, maintaining a sustainable pace of work, and fostering a collaborative and self-organizing team environment. These principles also emphasize the importance of technical excellence, simplicity, and regular reflection on how to become more effective.

Together, the values and principles of the Agile Manifesto form a cohesive framework that promotes a dynamic and user-focused approach to software development. By prioritizing collaboration, adaptability, and iterative progress, Agile methodologies enable teams to deliver high-quality products that meet user needs while navigating the complexities and uncertainties of modern projects.

Agile vs. Traditional Methodologies: Comparison with Waterfall and other traditional methods.

Agile and traditional methodologies, such as Waterfall, represent two distinct approaches to project management and software development, each with its own strengths and limitations. Understanding the differences between these methodologies is crucial for selecting the most appropriate approach based on the project's needs, complexity, and goals.

Waterfall, a traditional methodology, is characterized by its linear and sequential approach. In the Waterfall model, projects are divided into distinct phases: requirements gathering, design, implementation, testing, deployment, and maintenance. Each phase must be completed before the next begins, and changes are generally difficult to implement once a phase is finished. This structured approach is well-suited for projects with well-defined requirements and minimal expected changes, such as in construction or manufacturing. However, its rigidity can be a disadvantage in dynamic environments where requirements evolve or where iterative feedback is crucial.

In contrast, Agile methodologies prioritize flexibility, collaboration, and iterative progress. Agile methodologies, including Scrum, Kanban, and Extreme Programming (XP), involve iterative cycles or "sprints" where small, incremental pieces of the project are developed and delivered. This approach allows for frequent reassessment and adaptation based on user feedback and changing requirements. Agile is particularly advantageous in projects where requirements are expected to evolve, or where early and continuous delivery of valuable software is a priority. It encourages frequent communication among team members and stakeholders, fostering a collaborative environment that can quickly address issues and incorporate new insights.

Another traditional approach is Incremental Development, which, like Agile, breaks projects into smaller parts or increments. However, unlike Agile, which focuses on continuous improvement and flexibility, incremental development often follows a more predefined plan and is less adaptive to changes. The focus remains on delivering functional components in stages, but without the same emphasis on iterative feedback and frequent adjustments.

Agile vs. Traditional Methodologies often comes down to the nature of the project and the working environment. Agile methodologies offer significant advantages in terms of adaptability and responsiveness, making them ideal for fast-paced or complex projects where requirements are likely to change. Traditional methodologies, such as Waterfall, may be more effective in environments with clear, stable requirements where a structured, step-by-step approach is beneficial. By understanding the strengths and limitations of each methodology, organizations can choose the approach that best aligns with their project goals and operational context.

Chapter 2: Agile Frameworks and Methodologies

Scrum

Overview of Scrum.

Scrum is one of the most widely adopted Agile frameworks, designed to facilitate iterative and incremental development. It provides a structured yet flexible approach to managing complex projects, particularly in software development. Scrum emphasizes collaboration, accountability, and continuous improvement, making it an effective framework for teams looking to enhance their productivity and responsiveness.

At its core, Scrum divides projects into time-boxed iterations known as sprints, typically lasting two to four weeks. Each sprint begins with a Sprint Planning meeting, where the team selects a set of tasks from the Product Backlog—a prioritized list of features, enhancements, and bug fixes. The goal is to create a Sprint Backlog, a subset of the Product Backlog that the team commits to completing by the end of the sprint. This approach allows teams to deliver functional increments of the product regularly and receive feedback early and often.

Throughout the sprint, Scrum employs several key roles and ceremonies to ensure effective collaboration and progress. The Scrum Master facilitates the process, helps the team overcome obstacles, and ensures adherence to Scrum practices. The Product Owner represents the stakeholders and is responsible for prioritizing the Product Backlog, ensuring that the team focuses on delivering the most valuable features. The Development Team is composed of cross-functional members who work together to complete the tasks in the Sprint Backlog.

Daily progress is tracked through the Daily Scrum, a brief, time-boxed meeting where team members share updates on their work, discuss any impediments, and plan their tasks for the day. At the end of each sprint, the team conducts a Sprint Review to demonstrate the completed work to stakeholders and gather feedback. This is followed by a Sprint Retrospective, where the team reflects on the sprint, identifies areas for improvement, and discusses how to enhance their processes and performance in future sprints.

Scrum's iterative nature, combined with its focus on regular feedback and continuous improvement, makes it highly effective for managing complex projects where requirements are likely to evolve. By breaking work into manageable chunks and emphasizing collaboration and flexibility, Scrum helps teams deliver high-quality products while adapting to changing needs and priorities.

Roles (Scrum Master, Product Owner, Development Team).

In Scrum, the success of a project hinges on clearly defined roles and responsibilities. Each role plays a critical part in ensuring that the Scrum framework is applied effectively and that the team delivers high-quality results. The three primary roles in Scrum are the Scrum Master, the Product Owner, and the Development Team, each with distinct responsibilities and functions.

Scrum Master: The Scrum Master acts as a facilitator and servant leader for the Scrum team. Their primary responsibilities include:

- **Facilitating Scrum Events:** The Scrum Master organizes and ensures that Scrum events, such as Sprint Planning, Daily Scrums, Sprint Reviews, and Sprint Retrospectives, are conducted effectively.
- **Removing Impediments:** They work to identify and remove obstacles that may hinder the team's progress, helping to ensure that the Development Team can focus on delivering high-quality work.
- **Coaching and Mentoring:** The Scrum Master supports the team in understanding and applying Scrum principles and practices. They coach team members and stakeholders to embrace Agile values and foster a collaborative and self-organizing team environment.
- **Protecting the Team:** They act as a shield for the team against external distractions and interruptions, allowing team members to concentrate on their work and maintain a sustainable pace.

Product Owner: The Product Owner represents the interests of stakeholders and is responsible for maximizing the value delivered by the Scrum team. Their key responsibilities include:

- **Managing the Product Backlog:** The Product Owner creates, maintains, and prioritizes the Product Backlog, ensuring that it reflects the needs and priorities of stakeholders. They must make

decisions about what features and tasks should be worked on next based on business value and feedback.
- **Defining Requirements:** They clarify and communicate the requirements for the Product Backlog items, ensuring that the Development Team has a clear understanding of what needs to be built.
- **Engaging with Stakeholders:** The Product Owner regularly interacts with stakeholders to gather feedback, understand their needs, and ensure that the product meets their expectations. They act as the main point of contact for any questions or concerns related to the product.
- **Accepting Work:** They are responsible for reviewing and accepting or rejecting the work completed by the Development Team at the end of each sprint, based on whether it meets the Definition of Done and aligns with the acceptance criteria.

Development Team: The Development Team is composed of professionals who are responsible for delivering the product increment. Their main responsibilities include:

- **Delivering Value:** The Development Team works collaboratively to complete the tasks in the Sprint Backlog, delivering a potentially releasable product increment by the end of each sprint.
- **Self-Organization:** They are self-organizing, meaning they decide how to best accomplish their work without being directed by external sources. They are empowered to make decisions about how to approach tasks and solve problems.
- **Cross-Functionality:** The Development Team possesses all the skills necessary to complete the work within the sprint. This includes designing, developing, testing, and any other activities required to deliver the increment.
- **Maintaining Quality:** The Development Team ensures that the work adheres to the Definition of Done and meets quality standards. They are responsible for ensuring that each increment is potentially shippable and adds value to the product.

Each role in Scrum contributes to the overall success of the project by focusing on their specific responsibilities while working collaboratively to achieve the team's goals. The interplay between these roles helps create a productive and efficient Scrum environment, driving continuous improvement and delivering value to stakeholders.

Artifacts (Product Backlog, Sprint Backlog, Increment).

In Scrum, artifacts play a crucial role in managing and tracking the progress of a project. They provide transparency, facilitate communication, and help ensure that the Scrum team is aligned with the project goals. The three primary artifacts in Scrum are the Product Backlog, Sprint Backlog, and Increment, each serving a specific purpose in the Scrum framework.

Product Backlog: The Product Backlog is a dynamic, prioritized list of all the work needed to complete the project. It serves as a central repository for capturing everything that might be required in the product, including features, enhancements, bug fixes, and technical improvements. The key characteristics of the Product Backlog include:

- **Prioritization:** The Product Owner is responsible for ordering the items in the Product Backlog based on their value, importance, and urgency. Higher-priority items are addressed first, ensuring that the most valuable features are delivered early.
- **Emergent:** The Product Backlog is continuously updated and refined. As new information emerges, such as stakeholder feedback or market changes, items can be added, removed, or re-prioritized.
- **Detailing:** Items in the Product Backlog, known as Product Backlog Items (PBIs), vary in detail. High-priority items are often described in more detail, while lower-priority items may be less defined until they become more relevant.

Sprint Backlog: The Sprint Backlog is a subset of the Product Backlog, created during the Sprint Planning meeting. It consists of the items selected for the current sprint, along with a plan for delivering those items and achieving the sprint goal. The key characteristics of the Sprint Backlog include:

- **Commitment:** The Development Team commits to completing the items in the Sprint Backlog by the end of the sprint. This commitment reflects the team's understanding of what can be achieved within the sprint timeframe.
- **Sprint Goal:** The Sprint Backlog includes a Sprint Goal, which provides a clear objective for the sprint and helps guide the team's work and decision-making throughout the sprint.
- **Adaptability:** The Sprint Backlog is a living document that can be adjusted during the sprint. If the team encounters new information

or challenges, they may refine their approach or reallocate tasks as needed to achieve the Sprint Goal.

Increment: The Increment is the sum of all the Product Backlog Items completed during a sprint, combined with the increments from all previous sprints. It represents the current version of the product and must meet the Definition of Done. The key characteristics of the Increment include:

- **Potentially Shippable:** Each Increment is potentially shippable and should be in a state that could be released to users if needed. It must meet the quality standards and acceptance criteria defined in the Definition of Done.
- **Cumulative:** The Increment builds on previous increments, adding new functionality and improvements to the product. Each increment enhances the product's overall value and functionality.
- **Transparency:** The Increment provides a clear, tangible outcome of the team's work during the sprint. It allows stakeholders to see the progress made and provides an opportunity for feedback and review.

Together, these artifacts provide a structured approach to managing and tracking progress in Scrum. They ensure that the team remains focused on delivering value, adapting to changes, and continuously improving the product. By maintaining transparency and aligning with Scrum principles, the Product Backlog, Sprint Backlog, and Increment help facilitate successful project outcomes.

Events (Sprint, Sprint Planning, Daily Scrum, Sprint Review, Sprint Retrospective).

In Scrum, events provide a structured approach to managing and executing the work within each sprint. These events are designed to facilitate planning, communication, and continuous improvement. Here's an overview of each key Scrum event:

Sprint: A Sprint is a time-boxed iteration in which a set of work is completed and a potentially shippable product increment is delivered. Sprints typically last between two to four weeks, though the exact duration can be adjusted based on the team's needs. The key characteristics of a Sprint include:

- **Time-Boxed:** Sprints have a fixed duration, which helps maintain focus and urgency. This time-boxed approach ensures that teams deliver a consistent, predictable cadence of work.
- **Goal-Oriented:** Each Sprint is aimed at achieving a specific Sprint Goal, which is a concise statement of what the team aims to accomplish during the Sprint. This goal helps guide the team's efforts and align their work with project objectives.
- **Incremental:** At the end of the Sprint, the team produces a potentially shippable Increment of the product, which adds value and builds upon previous work.

Sprint Planning: Sprint Planning is the event where the team prepares for the upcoming Sprint. It occurs at the beginning of each Sprint and involves the entire Scrum Team. The key aspects of Sprint Planning include:

- **Defining the Sprint Goal:** The team collaborates to define a clear Sprint Goal that outlines the purpose and objectives of the Sprint. This goal helps focus the team's efforts and provides a shared understanding of what needs to be achieved.
- **Selecting Product Backlog Items:** The Product Owner presents the top-priority items from the Product Backlog, and the Development Team selects which items they can commit to completing during the Sprint. The team also breaks down these items into manageable tasks and creates the Sprint Backlog.
- **Planning the Work:** The team discusses and plans how to accomplish the selected items, including defining the work needed, identifying dependencies, and estimating effort.

Daily Scrum: The Daily Scrum, also known as the Daily Stand-up, is a short, time-boxed meeting held every day during the Sprint. It typically lasts 15 minutes and is attended by the Development Team, with the Scrum Master facilitating. The key elements of the Daily Scrum include:

- **Progress Updates:** Team members share updates on what they have accomplished since the last meeting, what they plan to work on next, and any obstacles they are facing.
- **Coordination:** The Daily Scrum helps the team coordinate their work, address any issues or impediments, and make adjustments to their plan if necessary.
- **Focus:** The meeting is designed to be concise and focused, ensuring that the team remains aligned and productive.

Sprint Review: The Sprint Review takes place at the end of the Sprint and involves the Scrum Team and stakeholders. Its purpose is to review the completed work and gather feedback. The key aspects of the Sprint Review include:

- **Demonstrating the Increment:** The Development Team presents the completed Increment to stakeholders, showcasing what has been achieved during the Sprint.
- **Gathering Feedback:** Stakeholders provide feedback on the Increment, discussing what they like, what could be improved, and any new requirements or changes.
- **Reviewing Progress:** The team and stakeholders discuss the progress of the project, review the Product Backlog, and make any necessary adjustments based on the feedback received.

Sprint Retrospective: The Sprint Retrospective is held after the Sprint Review and before the next Sprint Planning. It is a time for the Scrum Team to reflect on the Sprint and identify areas for improvement. The key components of the Sprint Retrospective include:

- **Reflecting on the Sprint:** The team discusses what went well, what didn't go well, and what could be improved. This reflection helps the team understand their performance and identify successes and challenges.
- **Identifying Improvements:** The team brainstorms and agrees on specific actions to address identified issues and enhance their processes. These actions are aimed at improving efficiency, quality, and collaboration.
- **Actionable Items:** The team creates a plan for implementing the identified improvements in the next Sprint, ensuring that they continuously refine their practices and processes.

These Scrum events work together to promote transparency, collaboration, and continuous improvement, helping teams deliver high-quality products efficiently while adapting to changes and feedback.

Kanban

Principles of Kanban.

Kanban is a popular Agile methodology designed to improve workflow and enhance efficiency by visualizing work, limiting work in progress (WIP), and focusing on continuous delivery. It provides a flexible approach to managing tasks and optimizing processes, making it particularly effective for teams and organizations that need to handle varying workloads and adapt to changing priorities.

Visualizing Work: One of the core principles of Kanban is visualizing work through a Kanban board. This board typically consists of columns that represent different stages of the workflow, such as "To Do," "In Progress," and "Done." Each task or work item is represented by a card that moves through these columns as it progresses. This visualization helps teams see the current state of work, identify bottlenecks, and ensure that everyone is aware of the status and flow of tasks. By providing a clear view of the workflow, Kanban enables better tracking, communication, and coordination among team members.

Limiting Work in Progress (WIP): Kanban emphasizes the importance of limiting work in progress to enhance focus and efficiency. By setting WIP limits for each column or stage of the workflow, teams ensure that they do not start new tasks until existing ones are completed. This helps prevent overloading team members, reduces multitasking, and minimizes the time tasks spend waiting in queues. Limiting WIP also aids in identifying and addressing bottlenecks in the workflow, allowing teams to streamline processes and improve overall productivity.

Managing Flow: Managing flow is another key principle of Kanban, focusing on optimizing the movement of work items through the workflow. The goal is to ensure a smooth, continuous flow of work, reducing delays and interruptions. Teams monitor metrics such as cycle time (the time it takes for a task to move from start to finish) to understand how efficiently work is progressing and to identify areas for improvement. By continuously analyzing and improving flow, Kanban helps teams deliver value more quickly and predictably.

Making Process Policies Explicit: Kanban encourages making process policies explicit and transparent. This involves clearly defining and documenting the rules, criteria, and guidelines that govern how work is managed and processed. Explicit process policies ensure that team members understand how tasks should be handled, what criteria must be met for work to move from one stage to another, and how to address common issues or exceptions. This clarity helps reduce confusion, improve consistency, and facilitate better decision-making.

Implementing Feedback Loops: Kanban integrates feedback loops to foster continuous improvement. Regular review meetings, such as retrospectives or reviews, allow teams to reflect on their processes, discuss what is working well, and identify areas for improvement. By incorporating feedback and making iterative adjustments, teams can refine their practices, adapt to changing needs, and enhance their overall performance.

Continuous Improvement: Kanban promotes a culture of continuous improvement by encouraging teams to regularly evaluate and optimize their processes. This principle involves making incremental changes based on feedback, performance data, and evolving needs. Continuous improvement helps teams stay agile and responsive, enhancing their ability to deliver high-quality work and adapt to new challenges.

Kanban's principles provide a flexible and visual approach to managing work, optimizing processes, and fostering a culture of continuous improvement. By focusing on visualization, WIP limits, flow management, explicit policies, feedback loops, and incremental changes, Kanban helps teams achieve greater efficiency, predictability, and responsiveness in their work.

Kanban Boards and Workflow Visualization.

Kanban boards are powerful tools used in project management and agile methodologies to visualize and manage workflows. Originating from Lean manufacturing principles, Kanban boards provide a clear, visual representation of work items as they progress through various stages of a process. Typically, a Kanban board is divided into columns that represent different stages of the workflow, such as "To Do," "In Progress," and "Done." Each work item is represented by a card, which moves across the columns as it progresses through the workflow. This visual representation helps teams see the status of each task at a glance, identify bottlenecks, and manage work more effectively.

Workflow visualization through Kanban boards offers several benefits. Firstly, it enhances transparency by making the entire workflow visible to all team members. This visibility fosters better communication and coordination, as everyone can see what others are working on and understand the overall progress of the project. Additionally, Kanban boards facilitate better prioritization and focus. By visualizing tasks and their status, teams can quickly identify high-priority items and ensure that they are addressed in a timely manner.

Moreover, Kanban boards support continuous improvement by making it easier to identify inefficiencies and areas for optimization. For example, if a particular stage of the workflow consistently becomes a bottleneck, teams can investigate and address the underlying issues, such as resource constraints or process inefficiencies. This iterative approach to workflow management helps teams adapt and refine their processes over time. Overall, Kanban boards and workflow visualization are essential tools for improving project management, enhancing team collaboration, and driving continuous improvement in various work environments.

WIP Limits and Continuous Delivery.

Work In Progress (WIP) limits are a fundamental concept in agile methodologies and Lean practices, particularly in Kanban. They restrict the number of tasks or items that can be in progress at any given time within a workflow. This constraint helps teams manage their workload more effectively, prevent bottlenecks, and ensure that tasks are completed before new ones are started. By focusing on a limited number of tasks, teams can improve their efficiency, maintain high quality, and reduce the time it takes to deliver work.

In the context of Continuous Delivery (CD), WIP limits play a crucial role in enhancing the overall software delivery process. Continuous Delivery is a practice that aims to automate and streamline the deployment pipeline, allowing teams to deliver updates and features to users more frequently and reliably. WIP limits contribute to CD by ensuring that the development process remains smooth and manageable. They help prevent overloading the system with too many simultaneous changes, which can lead to integration issues, longer feedback cycles, and delays in delivery.

By implementing WIP limits, teams can achieve a more predictable and sustainable pace of work, which aligns with the principles of Continuous Delivery. With fewer items in progress, teams can focus on completing each task thoroughly, leading to higher quality releases and a more efficient deployment pipeline. Additionally, WIP limits facilitate faster feedback by allowing teams to detect and address issues earlier in the process. This, in turn, supports the CD goal of delivering incremental improvements and maintaining a high level of agility and responsiveness to user needs. Overall, integrating WIP limits into the Continuous Delivery framework helps optimize workflow, reduce lead times, and enhance the overall effectiveness of the software delivery process.

Extreme Programming (XP)

Core Practices (Pair Programming, Test-Driven Development, Continuous Integration).

Extreme Programming (XP) is a software development methodology that emphasizes customer satisfaction, adaptability, and continuous improvement. It is known for its rigorous practices that aim to improve code quality and enhance team collaboration. Among the core practices of XP are Pair Programming, Test-Driven Development (TDD), and Continuous Integration, each contributing to the methodology's goal of delivering high-quality software efficiently.

Pair Programming involves two developers working together at one workstation. One developer, the "driver," writes the code, while the other, the "observer" or "navigator," reviews each line of code as it is written and provides guidance. This practice promotes real-time feedback, enhances code quality through continuous review, and facilitates knowledge sharing among team members. Pair Programming helps catch defects early, improves problem-solving, and fosters a collaborative team environment where skills and knowledge are distributed across the team.

Test-Driven Development (TDD) is a practice where developers write tests before writing the actual code. The cycle begins with writing a test case that defines a specific functionality or requirement. Then, developers write the minimum amount of code necessary to pass the test. Afterward, they refactor the code to improve its structure while ensuring that all tests continue to pass. TDD ensures that code is both testable and reliable from the outset, encourages simple design, and helps maintain a suite of tests that can quickly identify and prevent regressions.

Continuous Integration (CI) involves integrating code changes into a shared repository frequently, often several times a day. Each integration is automatically tested to detect integration issues early. CI practices ensure that new code changes are continuously validated against existing code, reducing integration problems and conflicts. This practice helps maintain a stable codebase, accelerates the development process, and facilitates a more efficient and collaborative workflow.

Together, these XP core practices support the methodology's emphasis on iterative development, high-quality code, and close collaboration between developers and stakeholders. By integrating Pair Programming, TDD, and Continuous Integration into their workflow, teams can enhance their ability to deliver reliable and maintainable software that meets customer needs effectively.

Benefits and Challenges of XP.

Benefits of Extreme Programming (XP)

1. **Improved Code Quality**: XP practices such as Test-Driven Development (TDD) and Pair Programming contribute significantly to high-quality code. TDD ensures that code is thoroughly tested and designed with testing in mind from the start. Pair Programming provides continuous code review, which helps in catching defects early and ensuring adherence to best practices.
2. **Enhanced Collaboration and Communication**: XP emphasizes frequent communication and collaboration among team members. Practices like Pair Programming and regular customer feedback sessions foster a strong team dynamic and ensure that everyone is aligned with the project's goals and requirements. This leads to better problem-solving and more cohesive team efforts.
3. **Faster Feedback and Adaptability**: By integrating code frequently through Continuous Integration (CI) and maintaining a close relationship with the customer, XP facilitates rapid feedback and iterative improvements. This allows teams to adapt quickly to changing requirements and address issues promptly, leading to a more responsive and flexible development process.
4. **Customer Satisfaction**: XP prioritizes customer involvement and feedback throughout the development process. Frequent releases and close collaboration with the customer ensure that the delivered product aligns well with their needs and expectations. This approach helps in delivering value early and often, enhancing overall customer satisfaction.

Challenges of Extreme Programming (XP)

1. **Steep Learning Curve**: XP requires teams to adopt and master several new practices and principles, which can be challenging, especially for those new to agile methodologies. Implementing practices like Pair Programming and TDD may require significant adjustments in team dynamics and development processes.
2. **Potential for Overhead**: Some XP practices, such as Pair Programming, can introduce additional overhead in terms of time and resources. For instance, while Pair Programming promotes high-quality code, it can initially slow down development speed as two developers work on the same task. Balancing this with productivity can be a challenge.
3. **Resistance to Change**: Teams accustomed to traditional development practices may resist adopting XP methodologies. Cultural and organizational resistance can hinder the successful implementation of XP practices, affecting overall effectiveness and buy-in from stakeholders.
4. **Continuous Customer Involvement Required**: XP relies heavily on continuous customer feedback and involvement, which may not always be feasible. If the customer is not consistently available or engaged, it can impact the ability to gather valuable feedback and make necessary adjustments, potentially affecting project outcomes.

Extreme Programming offers significant benefits in terms of code quality, team collaboration, and customer satisfaction. However, it also presents challenges related to learning new practices, managing potential overhead, and ensuring consistent customer engagement. Balancing these aspects is crucial for successfully implementing XP and achieving its intended outcomes.

Lean

Lean Principles.

Lean principles, originating from Lean manufacturing and the Toyota Production System, focus on optimizing processes, minimizing waste, and delivering maximum value to customers. These principles have been widely adapted across various industries, including software development, to enhance efficiency and effectiveness. The core principles of Lean include:

1. **Value**: Identify what is truly valuable to the customer and focus on delivering that value. Understanding customer needs and requirements is crucial for prioritizing work that directly contributes to customer satisfaction and business objectives. This principle helps ensure that every activity and task adds value from the customer's perspective.
2. **Value Stream**: Map out the entire value stream for each product or service, from initial concept to delivery. This involves analyzing all steps and processes involved in creating and delivering a product to identify and eliminate waste. By visualizing the value stream, organizations can pinpoint inefficiencies, bottlenecks, and areas for improvement.
3. **Flow**: Ensure a smooth and continuous flow of work through the value stream. By streamlining processes and removing obstacles, teams can reduce delays and improve overall efficiency. This principle emphasizes the importance of maintaining a steady workflow and minimizing interruptions that can impact productivity.
4. **Pull**: Implement a pull-based system where work is pulled through the process based on customer demand rather than pushing work through based on forecasts or schedules. This approach helps avoid overproduction and reduces the risk of excess inventory and resource waste. In software development, this might involve using Kanban boards to manage work in progress and prioritize tasks based on current needs.
5. **Perfection**: Continuously seek opportunities for improvement and strive for perfection. Lean principles emphasize the importance of incremental and continuous improvement through regular feedback and iterative enhancements. Teams are encouraged to adopt a culture of learning and experimentation to refine processes and achieve higher levels of efficiency and quality over time.

6. **Respect for People**: Foster a culture of respect and empowerment for employees. Lean principles highlight the importance of involving everyone in the improvement process and valuing their input and expertise. By empowering team members and encouraging collaboration, organizations can harness collective knowledge and drive more effective problem-solving and innovation.
7. **Eliminate Waste**: Identify and eliminate waste in all forms, including excess inventory, waiting time, unnecessary processes, and defects. Lean focuses on reducing activities that do not add value and optimizing resources to ensure that efforts are directed towards activities that contribute to the customer's needs and business goals.

By applying these Lean principles, organizations can enhance their efficiency, improve quality, and deliver greater value to customers. Lean methodologies promote a systematic approach to process optimization, continuous improvement, and waste reduction, making them valuable for achieving operational excellence across various domains.

Value Stream Mapping and Waste Reduction.

Value Stream Mapping (VSM) is a powerful tool used to visualize and analyze the flow of materials and information required to bring a product or service from conception to delivery. This technique helps organizations map out each step in their processes, identify inefficiencies, and uncover areas where value is added or wasted. The primary goal of VSM is to provide a comprehensive view of the entire value stream, enabling teams to understand how different activities contribute to or detract from the overall value delivered to the customer.

In Value Stream Mapping, the process is typically depicted through a series of diagrams that illustrate the flow of work, from the initial stages to final delivery. These maps often include various elements such as process steps, inventory levels, lead times, and information flows. By visualizing the value stream, organizations can pinpoint bottlenecks, delays, and unnecessary steps that hinder efficiency. This clarity allows teams to make informed decisions about where to focus their improvement efforts and prioritize changes that will have the most significant impact on overall performance.

Waste Reduction is a key focus of Lean methodologies and closely linked to Value Stream Mapping. Waste, in the context of Lean, refers to any activity or resource that does not add value to the customer and consumes time, money, or effort. By identifying and eliminating waste, organizations can streamline their processes, reduce costs, and improve quality. The seven traditional types of waste, often referred to as "muda," include overproduction, waiting, transport, extra processing, inventory, motion, and defects. Each type represents an area where improvements can be made to enhance efficiency and effectiveness.

Implementing waste reduction strategies involves analyzing the value stream to identify sources of waste and then applying Lean principles to address these issues. For example, by reducing excess inventory and minimizing waiting times, organizations can improve flow and reduce lead times. Similarly, eliminating unnecessary processing steps and simplifying workflows can enhance productivity and reduce costs. Waste reduction efforts are typically supported by practices such as continuous improvement (Kaizen), standardized work, and the use of visual management tools. Through these practices, organizations can foster a culture of ongoing refinement and efficiency, ultimately leading to greater customer satisfaction and operational excellence.

Lean and Agile Integration.

Integrating Lean and Agile methodologies offers a powerful approach to optimizing processes and delivering value in a more efficient and adaptive manner. Both methodologies share common principles, such as focusing on customer value, continuous improvement, and minimizing waste, but they apply these principles in slightly different ways. By combining Lean and Agile practices, organizations can enhance their ability to respond to change, improve quality, and streamline their workflows.

Lean emphasizes the elimination of waste and the optimization of processes to create more value for the customer. It focuses on streamlining operations, reducing lead times, and improving efficiency through techniques like Value Stream Mapping and waste reduction. Lean practices prioritize the identification and removal of non-value-adding activities, ensuring that every step in the process contributes to delivering value.

Agile, on the other hand, emphasizes iterative development, flexibility, and customer collaboration. Agile methodologies, such as Scrum and Kanban, promote adaptive planning and continuous delivery through short development cycles called sprints or iterations. Agile practices focus on responding to changing requirements, engaging customers in feedback, and delivering incremental value through frequent releases.

When Lean and Agile principles are integrated, organizations benefit from a holistic approach to process improvement and project management. Lean principles can be applied to enhance the efficiency of Agile processes by identifying and eliminating waste in workflows, thus accelerating delivery and improving quality. For instance, Lean techniques like Value Stream Mapping can help Agile teams visualize their workflows and identify bottlenecks or inefficiencies that may impact their ability to deliver features rapidly.

Conversely, Agile practices can complement Lean by providing a framework for iterative improvements and customer collaboration. Agile's focus on regular feedback and incremental progress aligns with Lean's goal of continuous improvement, allowing organizations to refine their processes and adapt quickly to changing customer needs. This synergy enhances the overall effectiveness of both methodologies, leading to more efficient workflows, better product quality, and increased customer satisfaction.

Integrating Lean and Agile methodologies enables organizations to leverage the strengths of both approaches, resulting in a more responsive, efficient, and value-driven development process. By combining Lean's focus on waste reduction with Agile's iterative and customer-centric approach, teams can achieve greater flexibility, enhance productivity, and deliver higher-quality products that meet evolving customer expectations.

Other Frameworks: Overview of additional frameworks like Crystal, DSDM, and FDD.

In addition to widely recognized methodologies like Scrum and Kanban, several other frameworks offer alternative approaches to project management and software development. These frameworks, including Crystal, Dynamic Systems Development Method (DSDM), and Feature-Driven Development (FDD), each bring unique perspectives and practices to the table, catering to different organizational needs and project contexts.

Crystal is a family of agile methodologies that emphasizes the importance of tailoring processes to the specific needs of a project and its team. Developed by Alistair Cockburn, Crystal focuses on the idea that there is no one-size-fits-all approach to software development. Instead, it advocates for selecting the appropriate methodology based on factors such as team size, project criticality, and complexity. Crystal methodologies range from Crystal Clear for small teams with low-risk projects to Crystal Red for larger, more complex projects. The core principles of Crystal include frequent delivery, reflective improvement, and close communication, with an emphasis on minimizing documentation and maximizing interpersonal interactions.

Dynamic Systems Development Method (DSDM) is a comprehensive agile framework that originated in the UK and is particularly well-suited for large-scale and complex projects. DSDM focuses on delivering business solutions through iterative development and active user involvement. The framework is structured around eight principles, including frequent delivery of products, active user involvement, and collaboration between all stakeholders. DSDM emphasizes the importance of maintaining a clear business focus and ensures that projects remain aligned with business objectives through regular reviews and prioritization of requirements. It also incorporates aspects of traditional project management, such as planning and risk management, making it a robust choice for organizations seeking a blend of agile and structured approaches.

Feature-Driven Development (FDD) is an agile methodology that prioritizes feature delivery and is particularly effective for larger teams and projects. Developed by Jeff De Luca and Peter Coad, FDD focuses on creating a model of the system, then iteratively developing and delivering features based on that model. The framework consists of five core activities: developing an overall model, building a feature list, planning by feature, designing by feature, and building by feature. FDD emphasizes the importance of delivering tangible, working features in short iterations and maintaining a well-defined scope of work. This approach helps ensure that projects deliver high-value features consistently and align with the overall system design.

Each of these frameworks—Crystal, DSDM, and FDD—offers distinct approaches to managing projects and delivering value. Crystal provides flexibility by adapting practices to project needs, DSDM integrates agile principles with traditional project management, and FDD emphasizes structured feature delivery. By understanding and leveraging these frameworks, organizations can choose the methodology that best fits their project requirements and team dynamics, ultimately enhancing their ability to deliver successful outcomes.

Chapter 3: Implementing Agile

Getting Started with Agile: Steps to initiate an Agile transformation.

Initiating an Agile transformation involves several key steps to ensure a smooth transition from traditional project management practices to Agile methodologies. Agile transformation is not just about adopting new tools or processes; it requires a shift in mindset, culture, and organizational practices. Here are the essential steps to get started with Agile:

1. **Assess Organizational Readiness**: Begin by evaluating your organization's readiness for Agile. This involves understanding the current state of your processes, culture, and team dynamics. Identify any existing challenges or pain points that Agile could address and assess the level of buy-in from leadership and key stakeholders. A readiness assessment helps in tailoring the transformation strategy to fit the specific needs of the organization.
2. **Define Clear Objectives and Goals**: Establish clear objectives and goals for the Agile transformation. These should align with your organization's strategic priorities and desired outcomes. Objectives might include improving time-to-market, enhancing collaboration, increasing customer satisfaction, or boosting team productivity. Defining these goals helps set a clear direction for the transformation and provides a benchmark for measuring success.
3. **Secure Executive Support**: Successful Agile transformation requires strong support from executive leadership. Ensure that senior management understands the benefits of Agile and is committed to supporting the change. Executive sponsors can provide the necessary resources, remove obstacles, and champion the transformation across the organization.
4. **Choose an Agile Framework**: Select an Agile framework or methodology that best fits your organization's needs. Popular frameworks include Scrum, Kanban, and Lean. Consider factors such as team size, project complexity, and organizational culture when choosing a framework. The selected framework will guide the implementation and adaptation of Agile practices.
5. **Develop a Transformation Plan**: Create a detailed transformation plan outlining the steps, timeline, and resources needed for the transition. The plan should include training and

coaching for teams, adjustments to existing processes, and the introduction of Agile practices and tools. Identify key milestones and establish a roadmap for implementing Agile across different teams or departments.
6. **Provide Training and Coaching**: Invest in training and coaching to equip teams with the skills and knowledge required for Agile practices. Training should cover Agile principles, methodologies, and specific frameworks chosen for the transformation. Coaching helps teams apply Agile practices effectively, overcome challenges, and continuously improve.
7. **Pilot Agile Practices**: Start with a pilot project or team to implement Agile practices on a smaller scale. This allows you to test the transformation approach, identify potential issues, and refine processes before scaling Agile across the organization. Use the insights gained from the pilot to make necessary adjustments and build confidence in the new approach.
8. **Foster a Culture of Continuous Improvement**: Agile transformation is an ongoing process that requires a culture of continuous improvement. Encourage teams to regularly reflect on their practices, gather feedback, and make iterative improvements. Emphasize the importance of collaboration, adaptability, and learning from failures as part of the Agile mindset.
9. **Scale Agile Practices**: Once the pilot phase demonstrates success, gradually scale Agile practices to other teams or departments. Ensure that the scaling process includes ongoing support, training, and adjustments based on lessons learned. Monitor progress, address challenges, and celebrate successes to maintain momentum and drive further adoption.
10. **Measure and Adjust**: Continuously measure the impact of the Agile transformation against the defined objectives and goals. Use metrics and feedback to assess the effectiveness of Agile practices, identify areas for improvement, and make necessary adjustments. Regularly review and refine the transformation strategy to ensure alignment with organizational goals and evolving needs.

By following these steps, organizations can effectively initiate an Agile transformation, enhance their ability to deliver value, and foster a culture of collaboration and continuous improvement.

Building an Agile Team: Roles, responsibilities, and team dynamics.

Building an Agile team involves more than just assembling a group of skilled individuals; it requires creating a cohesive unit with well-defined roles, clear responsibilities, and effective team dynamics. Agile teams are designed to be self-organizing and cross-functional, meaning that they possess a broad range of skills and collaborate closely to deliver value iteratively. Understanding the roles, responsibilities, and dynamics within an Agile team is crucial for fostering a productive and collaborative environment.

Roles and Responsibilities

In an Agile team, each role has specific responsibilities that contribute to the overall success of the project. Common roles include:

- **Product Owner**: The Product Owner is responsible for defining and prioritizing the product backlog, ensuring that the team works on the most valuable features and requirements. They act as the main point of contact for stakeholders, gathering feedback, and making decisions about the product's direction. The Product Owner ensures that the team delivers what the customer needs and maximizes the value of the product.
- **Scrum Master (in Scrum) or Agile Coach**: The Scrum Master or Agile Coach facilitates the Agile process, helping the team adhere to Agile principles and practices. They remove impediments, facilitate meetings, and support the team in maintaining effective workflows. The Scrum Master also works to ensure that the team continuously improves its processes and practices.
- **Development Team Members**: Development team members are responsible for designing, developing, testing, and delivering the product increment. They work collaboratively, using their diverse skills to complete tasks and achieve the goals set by the Product Owner. Team members are expected to be cross-functional, meaning they can contribute to various aspects of the project beyond their primary expertise.

Team Dynamics

Effective team dynamics are essential for an Agile team's success. Agile teams operate best in environments that foster open communication, collaboration, and mutual respect. Key aspects of positive team dynamics include:

- **Collaboration**: Agile teams thrive on collaboration, where team members actively share knowledge, ideas, and feedback. Regular communication and collaborative problem-solving help to ensure that everyone is aligned with the project's goals and can contribute to achieving them.
- **Empowerment**: Agile teams are self-organizing and empowered to make decisions about how to best accomplish their work. This empowerment encourages team members to take ownership of their tasks, innovate, and continuously improve their processes. Trust and autonomy are crucial for enabling team members to perform at their best.
- **Adaptability**: Agile teams must be adaptable and open to change. They are often faced with evolving requirements and changing priorities, and the ability to adjust quickly is vital for maintaining momentum and delivering value. Team members should be flexible and willing to pivot when necessary.
- **Continuous Improvement**: Agile teams are committed to continuous improvement, both in terms of their processes and their interactions. Regular retrospectives and feedback sessions provide opportunities for the team to reflect on their performance, identify areas for improvement, and implement changes to enhance their effectiveness.

Building an Agile team involves defining clear roles and responsibilities, fostering a collaborative and empowering environment, and maintaining a focus on continuous improvement. By understanding and implementing these elements, organizations can create high-performing Agile teams that deliver value efficiently and adapt to changing requirements with agility.

Agile Planning and Estimation: Techniques for planning sprints, user stories, and estimating work.

Effective planning and estimation are crucial for successful Agile project management. Agile methodologies emphasize flexibility and iterative progress, which requires precise and adaptive techniques for planning sprints, defining user stories, and estimating work. Here's an overview of key techniques used in Agile planning and estimation:

Sprint Planning

1. Sprint Planning Meeting: At the beginning of each sprint, the team holds a Sprint Planning Meeting to determine what work will be completed during the sprint. The meeting typically involves the Product Owner, Scrum Master, and development team. During this meeting, the Product Owner presents the prioritized items from the product backlog, and the team selects the items they can commit to completing based on their capacity.

2. Define Sprint Goals: The team establishes clear sprint goals that provide focus and direction for the work to be accomplished. Sprint goals help the team understand the purpose and expected outcomes of the sprint, ensuring alignment with the overall project objectives.

3. Break Down User Stories: The selected user stories are broken down into smaller, manageable tasks. This breakdown helps the team understand the scope of work and plan how to approach it within the sprint.

User Stories

1. Writing User Stories: User stories are brief, user-centered descriptions of features or functionality. They typically follow the format: "As a [user type], I want [a feature] so that [benefit]." User stories focus on the value delivered to the user and help ensure that the team understands the requirements from the user's perspective.

2. Acceptance Criteria: Each user story includes acceptance criteria that define the conditions under which the story is considered complete. Acceptance criteria provide clear expectations and help the team ensure that the delivered feature meets the required standards and functionality.

3. Prioritization: User stories are prioritized in the product backlog based on their value, urgency, and dependencies. The Product Owner works with stakeholders to prioritize stories, ensuring that the most valuable and important features are addressed first.

Estimating Work

1. Estimation Techniques:

- **Story Points**: Story points are a relative measure of the effort required to complete a user story. Teams assign story points based

on the complexity, effort, and uncertainty associated with each story. Common scales include Fibonacci numbers (e.g., 1, 2, 3, 5, 8, 13) or T-shirt sizes (e.g., XS, S, M, L, XL). Story points provide a way to estimate work without relying on exact time estimates.
- **Planning Poker**: Planning Poker is a consensus-based estimation technique where team members use cards to estimate the effort required for each user story. Each member independently selects a card representing their estimate, and then the team discusses and adjusts estimates until consensus is reached.
- **Ideal Days**: Some teams use ideal days to estimate how long a task would take if worked on continuously without interruptions. While less common in Agile, it can be useful in certain contexts to provide a time-based estimate.

2. Velocity: Velocity is a measure of the amount of work completed by the team in a sprint, typically expressed in story points. By tracking velocity over multiple sprints, the team can estimate their capacity for future sprints and plan accordingly.

3. Capacity Planning: Capacity planning involves assessing the available time and resources for a sprint. The team evaluates their capacity based on factors such as team member availability, holidays, and other commitments. This helps ensure that the planned work aligns with the team's actual ability to deliver.

Agile planning and estimation techniques involve iterative and adaptive processes that focus on delivering value and managing work effectively. By using techniques such as Sprint Planning Meetings, writing and prioritizing user stories, and employing various estimation methods, Agile teams can effectively plan sprints, manage workload, and ensure successful project outcomes.

Managing Backlogs: Creating and maintaining Product and Sprint Backlogs.

Effective backlog management is a cornerstone of Agile practices, ensuring that work is organized, prioritized, and ready for development. Both the Product Backlog and the Sprint Backlog play crucial roles in the Agile process, serving as dynamic tools to manage and track work.

Creating and Maintaining the Product Backlog

The **Product Backlog** is a prioritized list of features, enhancements, bug fixes, and other deliverables required for a product. It serves as the single source of truth for all the work needed to achieve the product vision. Creating and maintaining a Product Backlog involves several key activities:

1. **Initial Creation**: The Product Backlog is initially populated with items based on stakeholder input, user research, and project requirements. These items are typically expressed as user stories or features and should align with the product vision and strategic goals.
2. **Prioritization**: The Product Owner is responsible for prioritizing the backlog items based on their value, urgency, and dependencies. Prioritization ensures that the most valuable and critical work is addressed first. The Product Owner continuously reassesses priorities in response to changing business needs, customer feedback, and market conditions.
3. **Refinement**: The Product Backlog is a living document that requires ongoing refinement. This process, often referred to as backlog grooming or refinement, involves regularly reviewing and updating backlog items. Refinement includes clarifying requirements, breaking down large items into smaller, more manageable tasks, and re-evaluating priorities. This ensures that the backlog remains relevant and actionable.
4. **Stakeholder Engagement**: Engaging stakeholders is crucial for maintaining a well-defined Product Backlog. The Product Owner gathers feedback, aligns backlog items with stakeholder needs, and ensures that the backlog reflects the evolving goals and expectations of the project.

Creating and Maintaining the Sprint Backlog

The **Sprint Backlog** is a subset of the Product Backlog, representing the work that the team commits to completing during a specific sprint. It provides a detailed plan for the sprint and includes both the user stories selected for the sprint and the tasks required to complete them. Key activities in managing the Sprint Backlog include:

1. **Sprint Planning**: During the Sprint Planning Meeting, the team selects items from the Product Backlog to include in the Sprint Backlog. The selected items are based on their priority and the team's capacity for the upcoming sprint. The team also breaks these items down into actionable tasks, estimating the effort required for each task.

2. **Daily Updates**: The Sprint Backlog is actively managed throughout the sprint. Teams hold daily stand-up meetings to discuss progress, address obstacles, and update the Sprint Backlog as needed. This helps ensure that the team remains focused and adapts to any changes or new insights.
3. **Progress Tracking**: Progress is tracked using visual tools such as task boards or burndown charts. These tools provide a clear view of work completed, remaining tasks, and any potential issues that might impact the sprint's progress.
4. **Sprint Review and Retrospective**: At the end of each sprint, the team reviews the completed work and assesses whether the sprint goals were met. The Sprint Backlog is evaluated during the Sprint Review to determine if any items need further work or adjustment. Additionally, the team conducts a Sprint Retrospective to reflect on their performance, identify areas for improvement, and plan for future sprints.

Managing Product and Sprint Backlogs involves creating, prioritizing, and continuously refining these lists to ensure alignment with project goals and effective sprint planning. By maintaining a well-organized and prioritized backlog, teams can effectively manage their work, deliver valuable features, and adapt to changing requirements throughout the Agile process.

Chapter 4: Agile Practices

Daily Standups: Purpose and best practices.

Daily standups, also known as daily scrums, are a core practice in Agile methodologies, designed to foster communication and synchronization within a team. The primary purpose of a daily standup is to ensure that all team members are aligned on the project goals, understand what each person is working on, and identify any potential obstacles that may hinder progress. These brief, time-boxed meetings typically last around 15 minutes and are conducted standing up to keep them focused and concise.

To conduct an effective daily standup, it's crucial to adhere to several best practices. Firstly, the meeting should be held at the same time and place each day to build routine and consistency. Each participant should address three key questions: What did I accomplish yesterday? What am I working on today? Are there any blockers or issues affecting my work? This structure helps to streamline communication and ensures that all relevant information is shared.

Encouraging participation from all team members is vital for a successful standup. Team members should speak directly and concisely, avoiding long-winded explanations or problem-solving during the meeting. Instead, issues should be noted and addressed in separate discussions or follow-up meetings. Facilitators should keep the standup on track and ensure that the discussion remains focused on progress and impediments rather than diving into detailed problem-solving.

Finally, it's important to maintain a positive and collaborative atmosphere during the standup. The meeting should serve as a platform for support and coordination, rather than a forum for criticism. By fostering an environment of mutual respect and openness, daily standups can significantly enhance team cohesion and project momentum, helping teams adapt quickly to changes and stay on course toward their objectives.

Sprint Reviews and Retrospectives: How to conduct effective reviews and retrospectives.

Sprint Reviews and Retrospectives are crucial components of Agile methodologies, specifically Scrum, that help teams continually improve their processes and deliverables. These ceremonies not only provide a platform for assessing progress but also foster collaboration, transparency, and continuous improvement within the team.

Sprint Reviews are conducted at the end of each sprint and serve as a formal opportunity for the team to demonstrate the work completed during the sprint. To conduct an effective Sprint Review, it's essential to involve all relevant stakeholders, including product owners, team members, and sometimes customers. The primary goal is to showcase the increment of work that has been completed, gather feedback, and ensure alignment with the project's goals and stakeholder expectations. An effective Sprint Review should focus on what has been achieved, discuss any deviations from the planned work, and explore potential adjustments to the backlog based on feedback. It's important to maintain a positive and open atmosphere, encouraging constructive feedback and collaborative discussions about future priorities.

Sprint Retrospectives, on the other hand, are focused on improving team processes and performance. They are typically held after the Sprint Review and aim to reflect on the sprint's successes and challenges. To conduct a productive Retrospective, the team should follow a structured approach. Start by creating a safe environment where team members feel comfortable sharing their thoughts without fear of blame. Use various retrospective techniques, such as Start-Stop-Continue or the 4Ls (Liked, Learned, Lacked, Longed for), to guide the discussion. The team should focus on identifying actionable items that address any issues or inefficiencies encountered during the sprint. Setting clear and achievable goals for improvement and following up on these action items in subsequent sprints is crucial for the effectiveness of Retrospectives.

Both Sprint Reviews and Retrospectives are integral to the Agile framework, promoting transparency, continuous improvement, and team collaboration. By conducting these meetings effectively, teams can enhance their processes, adapt to changes, and ultimately deliver higher-quality products.

Continuous Integration and Continuous Delivery: Key concepts and practices.

Sprint Reviews and Retrospectives are integral ceremonies in Agile practices that help teams assess their progress and continuously improve their processes. Both serve distinct but complementary purposes in ensuring project success and fostering team growth.

Sprint Reviews are held at the end of each sprint to inspect the increment of work completed and adapt the product backlog as needed. To conduct an effective Sprint Review, start by preparing a clear agenda and inviting all relevant stakeholders, including team members, product owners, and key business representatives. During the review, demonstrate the work completed in the sprint, showcasing the new features or improvements to the product. Engage stakeholders by encouraging their feedback and discussing any adjustments needed for future sprints. Ensure that the review focuses on the increment's alignment with the sprint goals and the product vision. Document feedback and any changes to the product backlog, and update priorities based on the discussion.

Sprint Retrospectives follow the Sprint Review and provide an opportunity for the team to reflect on their processes and performance. The goal is to identify what went well, what could be improved, and how to implement changes in the next sprint. To conduct an effective Retrospective, create a safe and open environment where team members feel comfortable sharing their honest feedback. Use structured formats like Start-Stop-Continue or the 4Ls (Liked, Learned, Lacked, Longed for) to guide the discussion. Focus on actionable insights rather than dwelling on past mistakes. Facilitate the conversation to ensure everyone's voice is heard and prioritize improvement actions that the team can realistically implement. Document these actions and track their progress in subsequent sprints.

Both Sprint Reviews and Retrospectives should be time-boxed and goal-oriented to ensure they remain productive and efficient. Regularly conducting these ceremonies with a focus on openness, constructive feedback, and actionable outcomes can greatly enhance team performance, adaptiveness, and overall project success.

Test-Driven Development (TDD): Principles and benefits.

Test-Driven Development (TDD) is a software development methodology where tests are written before the actual code is developed. This approach emphasizes the creation of automated tests that define the desired behavior of a feature before coding begins. TDD revolves around a simple yet powerful cycle: write a test, run the test to see it fail, write the code to pass the test, and then refactor the code for improvement while ensuring all tests continue to pass.

The core principles of TDD include writing tests before implementation, focusing on one small piece of functionality at a time, and continually refactoring the codebase. By writing tests first, developers define clear and precise requirements for the code, which guides the development process and helps to prevent over-engineering. The iterative nature of TDD encourages developers to build only what is necessary to pass the tests, leading to cleaner and more efficient code. Additionally, the frequent refactoring step ensures that the code remains maintainable and adaptable to future changes.

The benefits of TDD are manifold. One significant advantage is the immediate feedback it provides. Since tests are written before the code, developers receive instant confirmation that their code meets the specified requirements, which helps catch defects early in the development cycle. This proactive approach to testing also improves code reliability and reduces the likelihood of bugs making it into production. Furthermore, the comprehensive test suite produced through TDD acts as a safety net, making it easier to refactor and extend the codebase with confidence, knowing that existing functionality is protected.

TDD promotes better design practices and a more disciplined development approach. By ensuring that every piece of code is tested and by fostering a focus on simplicity and clarity, TDD helps teams build robust and reliable software while enhancing their ability to respond to evolving requirements and maintain high-quality code over time.

Chapter 5: Agile Tools and Technologies

JIRA: Features and how to use it for Agile management.

JIRA is a popular project management tool developed by Atlassian, widely used for managing Agile projects. It offers a range of features that support various aspects of Agile management, including planning, tracking, and reporting.

Features of JIRA

1. **Issue Tracking**: JIRA provides robust issue tracking capabilities. Issues can represent tasks, bugs, stories, or any other type of work item. Each issue can be detailed with descriptions, attachments, comments, and custom fields.
2. **Agile Boards**: JIRA includes Kanban and Scrum boards, which are essential for visualizing and managing workflow. Scrum boards support sprint planning, backlog management, and sprint tracking, while Kanban boards are useful for continuous delivery processes and visualizing work in progress.
3. **Backlog Management**: The backlog management feature helps in prioritizing and grooming tasks. Teams can add, prioritize, and organize issues in the backlog, and move them into sprints as part of the planning process.
4. **Sprint Planning**: JIRA allows teams to plan and manage sprints. You can create and start sprints, assign issues to sprints, and track sprint progress with burndown charts and sprint reports.
5. **Reporting and Dashboards**: JIRA provides various reporting tools and customizable dashboards. You can generate reports such as burndown charts, velocity charts, and cumulative flow diagrams to analyze team performance and project progress.
6. **Custom Workflows**: JIRA supports customizable workflows to align with your team's processes. You can define different stages of work, transition rules, and statuses to match your Agile methodology.
7. **Integration**: JIRA integrates with numerous tools and platforms, including version control systems like Git, CI/CD tools, and other project management tools. This integration helps streamline development workflows and improves team collaboration.

Using JIRA for Agile Management

1. **Setting Up Projects**: Create a project in JIRA and choose the Agile template that best fits your needs, whether it's Scrum, Kanban, or another Agile framework. This setup will help tailor JIRA's features to your Agile practices.
2. **Creating and Managing Issues**: Start by creating issues for tasks, user stories, bugs, and other work items. Use issue types, priorities, and custom fields to categorize and detail each issue effectively.
3. **Building Backlogs**: Populate your backlog with issues and use JIRA's prioritization features to organize them. Regularly refine the backlog through grooming sessions to ensure that it reflects the current priorities and requirements.
4. **Planning Sprints**: Use the Scrum board to plan sprints. Drag and drop issues from the backlog into the sprint, set sprint goals, and start the sprint. JIRA will track the progress of the sprint and provide insights through sprint reports.
5. **Tracking Progress**: Utilize Agile boards to monitor work in progress. Kanban boards help visualize the flow of work, while Scrum boards show the progress of tasks within a sprint. Update issue statuses as work progresses to maintain accurate tracking.
6. **Generating Reports**: Leverage JIRA's reporting tools to gain insights into team performance and project status. Analyze burndown charts, velocity charts, and other reports to evaluate progress, identify trends, and make data-driven decisions.
7. **Customizing Workflows**: Tailor workflows to fit your team's processes. Define custom statuses, transitions, and rules to ensure that JIRA aligns with your Agile methodology and enhances your team's efficiency.

By leveraging these features and practices, JIRA can significantly enhance Agile project management, enabling teams to effectively plan, track, and deliver high-quality software.

Trello and Kanban Tools: Setting up Kanban boards.

Trello and other Kanban tools offer powerful methods for visualizing and managing workflows through Kanban boards, which are essential for streamlining project management and enhancing team productivity.

Setting up Kanban boards using these tools involves creating a clear, visual representation of tasks and workflows, making it easier for teams to track progress, prioritize work, and identify bottlenecks.

To set up a Kanban board in Trello or similar tools, start by creating a new board and defining the key stages of your workflow. These stages are typically represented as columns on the board, such as "To Do," "In Progress," and "Done." Each column represents a different phase in the task lifecycle, and tasks or work items are represented as cards that move through these columns as they progress. This visual approach helps teams quickly see the status of various tasks and understand the overall workflow at a glance.

Once the basic structure is established, populate the board with cards that represent individual tasks or work items. Each card can contain detailed information, such as descriptions, deadlines, attachments, and checklists. Assigning tasks to team members and setting due dates ensures that responsibilities are clear and deadlines are met. Many Kanban tools also allow for labels, tags, and priorities, which can further help in organizing and categorizing tasks based on their nature or urgency.

Kanban boards in tools like Trello offer flexibility and customization options, allowing teams to adapt the board to their specific needs. For example, teams can create additional columns for different stages of the workflow or use filters to focus on specific types of tasks. Additionally, Trello and other Kanban tools often integrate with other productivity apps, such as time tracking or communication tools, to further enhance workflow management.

Regularly updating and reviewing the Kanban board is crucial for maintaining an effective workflow. Teams should hold periodic meetings to discuss progress, address any obstacles, and adjust priorities as needed. This ongoing review helps ensure that the Kanban board remains an accurate and useful tool for managing tasks and supporting the team's goals.

Trello and other Kanban tools provide a visual and intuitive way to manage workflows through Kanban boards. By setting up columns to represent different stages, populating the board with detailed task cards, and regularly reviewing progress, teams can enhance their productivity and maintain a clear, organized approach to project management.

Version Control Systems (e.g., Git): Integration with Agile practices.

Version Control Systems (VCS) like Git are integral to modern software development, especially when integrated with Agile practices. Agile methodologies emphasize iterative development, continuous feedback, and flexibility, which align seamlessly with the functionalities offered by version control systems. Git, in particular, provides robust support for managing changes, coordinating team collaboration, and maintaining code integrity throughout the development lifecycle.

In Agile practices, where teams work in short sprints or iterations, Git facilitates seamless integration and delivery by allowing teams to manage code changes incrementally. Each sprint or iteration often involves multiple small changes, and Git's branching and merging capabilities make it easy to handle these changes without disrupting the main codebase. Developers can work on separate branches for features or bug fixes, and merge these branches back into the main branch after thorough testing and review. This supports Agile's focus on continuous integration and delivery by enabling frequent and reliable code updates.

Moreover, Git's support for collaboration and tracking complements Agile's emphasis on team communication and collaboration. Through features like pull requests, code reviews, and commit history, Git ensures that changes are well-documented and scrutinized before being integrated into the main codebase. This not only helps in maintaining code quality but also fosters transparency and collective ownership of the codebase, which are core principles of Agile.

Additionally, Git integrates well with various Agile tools and practices, such as continuous integration/continuous deployment (CI/CD) pipelines. Automated testing and deployment processes can be set up to trigger on specific Git events, such as commits or merges, ensuring that code changes are continuously tested and deployed. This supports Agile's goal of delivering value to customers quickly and efficiently, by automating repetitive tasks and reducing the risk of integration issues.

The integration of Git with Agile practices enhances the efficiency and effectiveness of the development process. Git's capabilities in managing code changes, supporting collaboration, and integrating with CI/CD pipelines align well with Agile principles, fostering a development environment that is both flexible and robust.

Collaboration Tools: Slack, Confluence, and other communication tools.

Collaboration tools like Slack, Confluence, and others play a crucial role in modern teamwork, enhancing communication, documentation, and project management across various organizational levels. Each tool brings unique features that contribute to a more streamlined and efficient work environment.

Slack is a popular communication tool designed for real-time messaging and collaboration. It facilitates team communication through channels, which can be organized by projects, departments, or topics. This structure helps keep conversations focused and easily searchable. Slack also supports direct messaging for private conversations, file sharing, and integrates with numerous other tools and services. Features like thread replies and @mentions help keep discussions organized and relevant. Slack's ability to integrate with project management tools, calendar apps, and various bots enhances its utility by centralizing notifications and automating routine tasks.

Confluence, on the other hand, is a collaboration and documentation tool that excels in creating and managing shared knowledge. It functions as a wiki where teams can document processes, project plans, meeting notes, and other important information. Confluence's hierarchical structure allows for organized spaces and pages, making it easy to navigate and find information. It supports collaborative editing, version control, and offers integration with other Atlassian tools like Jira, which can enhance project management and tracking. Confluence's robust search capabilities and templates streamline the creation of consistent and professional documentation.

Other communication and collaboration tools include **Microsoft Teams** and **Google Workspace**. Microsoft Teams integrates with Office 365 and offers features similar to Slack, such as chat, video meetings, and file sharing, with a strong focus on integration with Microsoft's suite of productivity tools. Google Workspace, which includes tools like Google Docs, Sheets, and Drive, provides cloud-based collaboration features that allow multiple users to work on documents simultaneously and maintain a shared drive for easy access to files and information.

Incorporating these tools into a collaborative workflow can significantly improve efficiency and communication. For instance, using Slack for instant messaging and real-time discussions, Confluence for detailed documentation and knowledge sharing, and integrating other tools for specific needs ensures that teams have a comprehensive suite of resources at their disposal. Regularly assessing the effectiveness of these tools and adapting their use to fit evolving team needs is essential for maintaining an optimal collaborative environment.

Slack, Confluence, and other communication tools provide a range of functionalities that support effective teamwork, from real-time communication to detailed documentation, helping organizations stay organized and productive.

Chapter 6: Scaling Agile

Scaling Frameworks: Overview of SAFe, LeSS, and Spotify Model.

Scaling frameworks like SAFe, LeSS, and the Spotify Model offer structured approaches to apply Agile practices across larger organizations or multiple teams. Each framework addresses the challenges of scaling Agile by providing specific guidelines and practices tailored to different organizational needs and structures.

SAFe (Scaled Agile Framework)

SAFe is a comprehensive framework designed to scale Agile practices across large enterprises. It provides a detailed structure for implementing Agile at various levels, including team, program, and portfolio. SAFe introduces the concept of the Agile Release Train (ART), which is a long-lived team of Agile teams that work together to deliver value in a synchronized manner. This framework emphasizes alignment, collaboration, and delivery through a series of well-defined roles, ceremonies, and artifacts.

Key aspects of SAFe include:

- **Program Increment (PI) Planning:** A cadence-based event where teams plan and commit to work for a set period (usually 8-12 weeks). This ensures alignment and coordination among teams.
- **Roles and Artifacts:** SAFe introduces roles like Release Train Engineer (RTE) and Product Management, and artifacts such as the Program Backlog and PI Objectives.
- **Portfolio Management:** It provides a structured approach for aligning business strategy with execution, using portfolio backlogs and Lean budgeting.

SAFe is known for its prescriptive nature, which helps organizations implement Agile practices with a high degree of structure and support. It is suitable for large organizations looking for a robust and detailed framework to scale Agile across multiple teams and departments.

LeSS (Large Scale Scrum)

LeSS is a lightweight framework that extends Scrum principles to large-scale operations while maintaining simplicity. It focuses on applying Scrum principles at scale without introducing complex layers of processes. LeSS builds upon the foundational Scrum practices and adapts them for multiple teams working on the same product.

Key aspects of LeSS include:

- **One Product Backlog:** Unlike SAFe, LeSS promotes the use of a single Product Backlog for all teams working on the product, which helps maintain a unified vision and priorities.
- **Sprint Planning:** Teams coordinate their work through a common Sprint Planning event, ensuring alignment across the entire product.
- **Role of the Product Owner:** LeSS maintains a single Product Owner responsible for the overall product backlog, supported by a team of Product Owners if needed.

LeSS is designed for organizations that want to scale Scrum without adding unnecessary complexity. It emphasizes minimalism and the application of Scrum principles at a larger scale, making it suitable for companies already familiar with Scrum practices.

Spotify Model

The Spotify Model, developed by Spotify, is more of an organizational culture and structure framework rather than a prescriptive methodology. It focuses on creating a culture of innovation, autonomy, and alignment by organizing teams into "squads," "tribes," "chapters," and "guilds."

Key aspects of the Spotify Model include:

- **Squads:** Autonomous teams responsible for specific features or services. Each squad operates like a mini-startup with its own mission and goals.
- **Tribes:** Groups of squads that work on related areas of the product or business. Tribes ensure coordination and collaboration among squads.
- **Chapters:** Functional groups within tribes that provide expertise and best practices. Chapters help maintain consistency and knowledge sharing across squads.

- **Guilds:** Cross-functional communities of interest that span across tribes and chapters, fostering innovation and shared learning.

The Spotify Model emphasizes team autonomy and alignment with the broader organizational goals. It is less about specific practices and more about fostering a culture that supports Agile principles and continuous improvement.

SAFe, LeSS, and the Spotify Model offer different approaches to scaling Agile practices. SAFe provides a comprehensive and structured framework for large enterprises, LeSS focuses on scaling Scrum with minimal complexity, and the Spotify Model emphasizes culture and organizational structure to support Agile practices. Choosing the right framework depends on an organization's size, complexity, and existing Agile maturity.

Challenges in Scaling Agile: Common issues and solutions.

Scaling Agile across larger teams or organizations often brings a set of challenges that can impact the effectiveness of Agile practices. Here are some common issues faced in scaling Agile and potential solutions to address them:

1. Coordination Across Teams

Challenge: As teams grow in number and work on different aspects of a project, coordinating their efforts becomes complex. Dependencies between teams can lead to delays and misalignment.

Solution: Implementing frameworks like SAFe or LeSS can provide structured approaches to managing dependencies and coordination. Techniques such as regular cross-team synchronization meetings, such as Scrum of Scrums, can help teams align their work. Additionally, using a common backlog and shared goals ensures that all teams are working towards the same objectives.

2. *Maintaining Consistency*

Challenge: Scaling Agile often involves maintaining consistency in practices, standards, and communication across multiple teams.

Different teams might interpret Agile principles differently, leading to variations in how processes are applied.

Solution: Establish clear guidelines and standards for Agile practices across the organization. Provide training and coaching to ensure that all teams are aligned in their understanding and application of Agile principles. Tools like Confluence can be used to document and share best practices, ensuring consistency.

3. Managing Complex Dependencies

Challenge: In larger Agile environments, managing dependencies between teams or projects can become cumbersome, potentially causing delays and bottlenecks.

Solution: Use tools and techniques for dependency management, such as visualizing dependencies on Kanban boards or using project management tools that highlight inter-team dependencies. Agile frameworks like SAFe offer specific practices for managing dependencies, such as PI Planning, which brings together teams to plan and align their work.

4. Scaling Communication

Challenge: Effective communication becomes more challenging as the number of teams increases. Important information might not reach all relevant parties, leading to misunderstandings and inefficiencies.

Solution: Utilize communication tools like Slack or Microsoft Teams to facilitate real-time communication and collaboration. Regularly scheduled cross-team meetings and updates help ensure that information is shared across the organization. Implementing a centralized information repository, such as Confluence, can also help in disseminating important updates and documents.

5. Aligning with Organizational Goals

Challenge: Ensuring that all teams are aligned with the broader organizational goals and strategy can be difficult when scaling Agile practices.

Solution: Align team goals with organizational objectives by using frameworks that emphasize alignment, such as SAFe. Regularly review and adjust team backlogs to reflect changes in organizational priorities.

Ensure that leaders communicate the organization's vision and goals clearly and frequently.

6. Resource Allocation

Challenge: Properly allocating resources, including personnel and budget, across multiple teams can be challenging and may lead to conflicts or inefficiencies.

Solution: Implement portfolio management practices to ensure that resources are allocated effectively. Use tools and techniques for tracking and managing resource utilization, and make data-driven decisions to adjust allocations as needed. Agile frameworks like SAFe include portfolio management practices to help address these challenges.

7. Cultural Resistance

Challenge: Scaling Agile may face resistance from individuals or teams accustomed to traditional practices or skeptical of Agile methods.

Solution: Foster a culture of change by providing training and demonstrating the benefits of Agile practices. Engage leaders and champions who can advocate for Agile and address concerns. Gradual adoption, starting with pilot teams, can help in demonstrating value and gaining buy-in.

8. Balancing Autonomy and Control

Challenge: Scaling Agile involves balancing team autonomy with the need for oversight and control to ensure alignment and consistency.

Solution: Define clear boundaries for team autonomy while maintaining oversight through regular reviews and alignment meetings. Use frameworks that promote both autonomy and alignment, such as the Spotify Model, which allows teams to operate independently while staying connected through tribes and chapters.

Scaling Agile presents several challenges, from coordination and consistency to communication and cultural resistance. Addressing these challenges requires a combination of structured frameworks, effective tools, and cultural change initiatives. By implementing best practices and solutions tailored to their specific needs, organizations can successfully scale Agile practices and achieve greater efficiency and alignment across their teams.

Case Studies: Examples of organizations that successfully scaled Agile.

Scaling Agile effectively can be challenging, but several organizations have successfully navigated this journey, demonstrating how Agile practices can be expanded to larger teams and complex projects. Here are a few notable case studies:

1. *Spotify*

Context: Spotify, the music streaming giant, is known for its unique approach to scaling Agile. The company had a rapidly growing team and needed to maintain a high level of innovation and efficiency.

Approach: Spotify adopted a model that emphasizes autonomous squads, chapters, and guilds. Squads are cross-functional teams responsible for specific features or products, while chapters are groups of individuals with similar skills across squads, and guilds are broader communities of practice focused on specific topics.

Outcome: This model has allowed Spotify to maintain a high level of flexibility and innovation while scaling. The emphasis on autonomy and alignment with company goals has helped Spotify deliver new features and improvements quickly, fostering a strong culture of collaboration and continuous learning.

2. *ING Bank*

Context: ING Bank, a major global financial institution, sought to improve its agility and responsiveness to market changes.

Approach: ING adopted the Scaled Agile Framework (SAFe) to scale Agile across its organization. The bank implemented Agile at the team level and extended it to the program and portfolio levels, focusing on aligning Agile practices with business objectives.

Outcome: ING successfully improved its speed to market and overall responsiveness. The bank reported enhanced collaboration between teams, more effective prioritization of work, and increased customer satisfaction. The SAFe implementation helped ING align Agile practices with its broader strategic goals.

3. *Cisco*

Context: Cisco, a global technology leader, aimed to improve its product development processes and enhance collaboration across its teams.

Approach: Cisco implemented Agile practices using the Scrum framework and extended Agile across multiple teams and departments. The company also incorporated DevOps practices to improve continuous integration and delivery.

Outcome: Cisco achieved significant improvements in its development cycles, including faster delivery times and higher quality releases. The Agile transformation also fostered better communication and collaboration between development and operations teams, leading to more streamlined and efficient processes.

4. Capital One

Context: Capital One, a major financial services company, needed to modernize its technology stack and improve its ability to respond to customer needs.

Approach: Capital One embraced Agile and DevOps practices across its technology teams, focusing on building a culture of experimentation and continuous improvement. The company adopted Agile methodologies at scale using frameworks like SAFe and integrated them with DevOps to enhance delivery and collaboration.

Outcome: Capital One successfully accelerated its software delivery process, improved its ability to deploy new features, and enhanced overall product quality. The combination of Agile and DevOps practices allowed Capital One to become more responsive to customer demands and market changes.

5. GE Healthcare

Context: GE Healthcare aimed to improve its product development processes and accelerate the delivery of medical technologies.

Approach: GE Healthcare adopted Agile practices and scaled them across its global teams. The company used a mix of Scrum and Kanban frameworks to manage projects and implemented Agile at both the team and program levels.

Outcome: GE Healthcare reported faster development cycles, improved collaboration, and more efficient processes. The Agile transformation helped the company bring new medical technologies to market more quickly, enhancing its ability to meet healthcare needs and stay competitive.

6. IBM

Context: IBM, a technology and consulting company, sought to improve its software development processes and adapt to a rapidly changing market.

Approach: IBM implemented Agile practices using the SAFe framework to scale Agile across its development teams. The company focused on aligning Agile practices with its broader business objectives and integrated Agile with its existing project management processes.

Outcome: IBM experienced improved project visibility, faster delivery times, and enhanced collaboration between teams. The scaling of Agile practices helped IBM better manage complex projects and respond more effectively to customer needs and market shifts.

These case studies illustrate that with careful planning, a clear vision, and strong leadership, organizations can successfully scale Agile practices to drive significant improvements in efficiency, collaboration, and responsiveness.

Chapter 7: Measuring Agile Success

Key Performance Indicators (KPIs): Metrics for Agile success.

Key Performance Indicators (KPIs) are crucial for measuring the success of Agile initiatives, as they provide quantifiable metrics that help teams and organizations assess their performance and progress. KPIs in Agile are designed to evaluate various aspects of Agile practices, including team efficiency, delivery quality, and overall alignment with business goals. By focusing on relevant KPIs, organizations can identify areas for improvement, make informed decisions, and drive continuous enhancement in their Agile processes.

Velocity is one of the most common KPIs in Agile, particularly in Scrum. It measures the amount of work a team completes during a sprint, typically quantified in story points or effort estimates. Tracking velocity over time helps teams understand their capacity and forecast future work. This metric is valuable for assessing how well teams are performing relative to their planned work and can highlight trends or changes in productivity.

Cycle Time is another important KPI that tracks the time it takes for a work item to move from the beginning of the development process to completion. This metric helps in evaluating the efficiency of the development process and identifying bottlenecks. Reducing cycle time often leads to faster delivery of features and improved responsiveness to customer needs.

Lead Time measures the total time taken from the moment a feature request is made until it is delivered. It provides insight into how quickly teams can turn ideas into completed work. Lead time is particularly useful for understanding the end-to-end process and identifying areas where delays occur, enabling teams to streamline their workflows.

Defect Rate assesses the number of defects or bugs reported after a feature is released. This KPI helps teams gauge the quality of their deliverables and the effectiveness of their testing practices. A high defect rate might indicate issues with the development or testing processes, prompting a review and improvement of quality assurance practices.

Customer Satisfaction can be measured through metrics such as Net Promoter Score (NPS) or customer feedback surveys. This KPI reflects how well the delivered product or feature meets customer expectations and needs. High customer satisfaction indicates that the Agile practices are effectively aligning with customer requirements and delivering value.

Team Happiness or employee satisfaction is another KPI that measures the morale and engagement of team members. Happy and engaged teams are often more productive and collaborative. Regular surveys or feedback mechanisms can provide insights into team dynamics and areas where support or improvements might be needed.

Burn Down Charts visually track the progress of work remaining in a sprint or project. They provide a clear picture of whether the team is on track to complete their work by the end of the sprint or release cycle. Monitoring burn down charts helps in assessing progress and adjusting plans as necessary.

KPIs for Agile success provide valuable insights into various aspects of Agile performance, from team productivity and process efficiency to product quality and customer satisfaction. By selecting and monitoring relevant KPIs, organizations can drive continuous improvement, ensure alignment with goals, and ultimately enhance their Agile practices.

Feedback Loops: How to gather and utilize feedback.

Feedback loops are fundamental in various domains, from product development to organizational growth, as they help organizations continuously refine and improve their offerings based on real-world input. A feedback loop involves collecting input from stakeholders, analyzing it, and using the insights gained to make informed adjustments. This iterative process ensures that products or services align more closely with user needs and expectations, fostering continuous improvement.

Gathering feedback effectively starts with identifying the right sources of input. For product development, this often involves engaging directly with users through surveys, interviews, or usability testing. For internal processes, feedback might come from team members or other departments through regular check-ins, retrospectives, or performance reviews. It's important to create channels that make it easy for individuals to provide honest and constructive feedback. Tools like feedback forms, suggestion boxes, and digital platforms can facilitate this process. Additionally, fostering a culture that values and encourages feedback ensures that the information gathered is both relevant and actionable.

When it comes to internal processes, feedback might originate from within the organization, particularly from team members or other departments. Regular check-ins, retrospectives, and performance reviews are common avenues for collecting this type of feedback. These sessions allow team members to reflect on what's working, what's not, and how processes can be improved. Creating a safe and open environment for these discussions encourages honesty and constructive criticism, which are vital for continuous improvement.

To streamline the feedback-gathering process, it's essential to establish easy-to-use channels that facilitate honest input. Tools like feedback forms, suggestion boxes, and digital platforms can be instrumental in this regard. These tools provide accessible ways for individuals to share their thoughts, whether they prefer to do so anonymously or openly. Furthermore, fostering a culture that values and encourages feedback is key to making these channels effective. When team members and users alike feel that their feedback is valued and will be acted upon, they are more likely to provide thoughtful and meaningful input, ultimately driving improvements in both products and processes.

Utilizing feedback involves a systematic approach to analyzing and implementing the insights gained. Once feedback is collected, it should be categorized and prioritized based on factors such as impact, feasibility, and alignment with strategic goals. Engaging in this analysis helps identify common themes or recurring issues that need addressing. The next step is to incorporate the feedback into actionable plans, which might involve making design changes, adjusting strategies, or improving processes. Communicating the changes made as a result of the feedback loop is also crucial, as it demonstrates responsiveness and helps build trust with stakeholders. Regularly reviewing the outcomes of implemented changes ensures that the feedback loop remains effective and that continuous improvements are sustained over time.

Utilizing feedback effectively requires a systematic approach that begins with thorough analysis and thoughtful implementation. After collecting feedback, it's crucial to categorize and prioritize the insights based on their potential impact, feasibility, and alignment with the organization's strategic goals. This prioritization allows teams to focus on the most significant and actionable areas, ensuring that efforts are directed where they can make the most meaningful difference. By identifying common themes or recurring issues, teams can address underlying problems rather than just surface-level symptoms, leading to more sustainable improvements.

The next step in utilizing feedback is to translate the insights into actionable plans. This could involve making specific design changes to a product, adjusting broader strategies to better meet user or business needs, or refining internal processes to improve efficiency and effectiveness. The key here is to move from analysis to action swiftly, ensuring that the feedback loop doesn't stagnate. When feedback is promptly addressed and integrated into tangible changes, it not only improves the end product or process but also signals to stakeholders that their input is valued and taken seriously.

Equally important is the communication of the changes made as a result of the feedback. This transparency builds trust with stakeholders, whether they are customers, employees, or partners, by showing that their voices have a direct impact. It also reinforces a culture of continuous improvement, where feedback is not just collected but actively used to drive positive change. Finally, regularly reviewing the outcomes of these implemented changes is essential to maintaining an effective feedback loop. Continuous monitoring ensures that the adjustments are delivering the desired results and provides further opportunities to refine and enhance processes over time, creating a dynamic cycle of ongoing improvement.

Feedback loops are essential for driving progress and achieving excellence. By systematically gathering, analyzing, and acting on feedback, organizations can enhance their products, refine their processes, and better meet the needs of their users and stakeholders.

Continuous Improvement: Techniques for ongoing enhancement.

Continuous improvement is a fundamental principle of Agile and Lean methodologies, emphasizing the ongoing refinement of processes, products, and performance to achieve better results and greater efficiency. Techniques for continuous improvement focus on iterative enhancements, learning from past experiences, and actively seeking ways to optimize various aspects of work. Here are several key techniques for fostering continuous improvement:

1. **Iterative Reviews and Retrospectives:** Regularly scheduled reviews and retrospectives are central to the continuous improvement process. In Agile frameworks like Scrum, retrospectives are held at the end of each sprint to reflect on what went well, what could be improved, and actionable steps for enhancement. This practice encourages teams to openly discuss challenges, celebrate successes, and identify areas for improvement. By iterating on feedback and implementing improvements, teams can continuously refine their processes and performance.

2. **Data-Driven Decision Making:** Leveraging data and metrics is essential for informed decision-making and continuous improvement. Techniques such as tracking key performance indicators (KPIs), analyzing cycle times, and monitoring defect rates provide valuable insights into performance trends and areas needing attention. Data-driven approaches enable teams to make objective decisions, identify bottlenecks, and prioritize improvements based on evidence rather than intuition.

3. **Kaizen Principles:** Originating from Lean manufacturing, Kaizen emphasizes small, incremental changes that lead to significant long-term improvements. The philosophy of continuous, small-scale improvements encourages all team members to contribute ideas and suggestions for enhancing processes, reducing waste, and increasing efficiency. Implementing Kaizen involves regular, structured reviews of processes and the adoption of small, actionable changes that collectively drive ongoing enhancement.

4. **Root Cause Analysis:** Identifying and addressing the root causes problems is crucial for effective continuous improvement. Techniques like the "Five Whys" or fishbone diagrams (Ishikawa diagrams) help teams investigate the underlying causes of issues rather than just addressing symptoms. By understanding and resolving root causes, teams can implement more effective solutions and prevent recurring problems.

5. **Experimentation and A/B Testing:** Experimentation involves testing new approaches or changes on a small scale before full-scale implementation. Techniques like A/B testing allow teams to compare the impact of different variations and make data-driven decisions about which approach yields better results. This iterative experimentation fosters a culture of innovation and helps teams discover more effective methods and solutions.

6. **Feedback Mechanisms:** Regularly gathering feedback from stakeholders, customers, and team members is vital for continuous improvement. Surveys, interviews, and user feedback sessions provide insights into how well processes and products are meeting needs and expectations. Incorporating feedback into the improvement process ensures that changes are aligned with user requirements and business goals.

7. **Learning and Development:** Investing in ongoing training and professional development supports continuous improvement by keeping team members updated on new techniques, tools, and best practices. Encouraging a culture of learning and knowledge sharing promotes skill enhancement and fosters an environment where continuous improvement is a shared responsibility.

8. **Automated Testing and Continuous Integration: In software development, automated testing and continuous integration are crucial for maintaining high quality and efficiency. Automated tests help catch defects early, while continuous integration ensures that code changes are regularly integrated and tested. These practices contribute to a more reliable and agile development process, allowing teams to quickly address issues and implement improvements.

By employing these techniques, organizations can create a culture of continuous improvement that drives ongoing enhancement and adaptation. Emphasizing iterative refinement, data-driven decision-making, and collaborative feedback ensures that teams and processes remain responsive, efficient, and aligned with evolving goals and challenges.

Chapter 8: Agile and Organizational Culture

Creating an Agile Culture: Principles for fostering an Agile mindset.

Creating an Agile culture involves fostering an environment where Agile principles and practices are deeply ingrained in daily operations, behaviors, and attitudes. This cultural shift is crucial for achieving the full benefits of Agile methodologies and ensuring that teams are adaptable, collaborative, and focused on delivering value. Here are key principles for fostering an Agile mindset within an organization:

1. Embrace Continuous Learning and Adaptability

An Agile culture thrives on continuous learning and the ability to adapt to change. Encourage teams to view every challenge as an opportunity for growth and improvement. Promote a mindset of experimentation, where failure is seen as a learning opportunity rather than a setback. Provide opportunities for training, knowledge sharing, and professional development to help team members stay current with Agile practices and industry trends.

2. Foster Open Communication and Collaboration

Open communication and collaboration are foundational to an Agile culture. Encourage transparency and frequent communication among team members, stakeholders, and leaders. Create an environment where feedback is welcomed and acted upon, and where team members feel comfortable sharing their ideas and concerns. Collaborative tools and practices, such as regular stand-ups, retrospectives, and cross-functional teams, support this principle.

3. Empower Teams and Promote Autonomy

Empowering teams to make decisions and take ownership of their work is crucial for fostering an Agile mindset. Provide teams with the autonomy to manage their tasks and make decisions related to their work. Encourage self-organizing teams that are capable of solving problems and adapting to changes without waiting for top-down directives. Support this autonomy with clear goals and regular alignment with broader organizational objectives.

4. Prioritize Customer Value and Feedback

An Agile culture places a strong emphasis on delivering value to customers and incorporating their feedback. Encourage teams to focus on understanding customer needs and prioritizing features that provide the most value. Implement practices such as user stories, customer feedback sessions, and iterative releases to ensure that the product evolves based on real customer insights and requirements.

5. Promote a Culture of Trust and Psychological Safety

Creating a culture of trust and psychological safety is essential for enabling teams to thrive in an Agile environment. Encourage a supportive atmosphere where team members feel safe to express their ideas, take risks, and admit mistakes without fear of blame or retribution. This trust fosters creativity, collaboration, and innovation, and is critical for effective teamwork and problem-solving.

6. Lead by Example

Leadership plays a crucial role in shaping an Agile culture. Leaders should model Agile behaviors and principles by embracing change, being transparent, and supporting continuous improvement. Leadership commitment to Agile practices helps reinforce the importance of these principles and sets a positive example for teams to follow.

7. Align with Organizational Goals and Vision

For Agile practices to be effective, they must be aligned with the organization's overall goals and vision. Ensure that Agile initiatives and practices support the strategic objectives of the organization and are integrated into the broader business context. Regularly communicate how Agile practices contribute to achieving organizational goals and drive value.

8. Encourage Cross-Functional Teams

Agile promotes cross-functional teams that bring together diverse skills and perspectives to address complex challenges. Encourage the formation of cross-functional teams that can collaborate effectively and leverage their collective expertise. This approach enhances problem-solving capabilities and promotes a holistic view of the work being done.

9. Celebrate Successes and Recognize Contributions

Recognizing and celebrating successes, both big and small, reinforces positive behavior and motivates teams to continue striving for excellence. Celebrate achievements, milestones, and innovative solutions to create a positive and encouraging work environment. Recognizing individual and team contributions helps build morale and reinforces the value of Agile practices.

10. *Continuously Reflect and Improve*

Agile is inherently about continuous improvement. Regularly reflect on team performance, processes, and practices to identify areas for enhancement. Use retrospectives and feedback loops to evaluate what is working well and what can be improved. Encourage a culture where reflection and improvement are ongoing and integral to the team's workflow.

By applying these principles, organizations can create a robust Agile culture that supports adaptability, collaboration, and continuous improvement. This cultural shift is essential for realizing the full potential of Agile methodologies and achieving sustained success in a dynamic and rapidly changing environment.

Leadership in Agile: Role of leaders in Agile transformations.

Leadership plays a crucial role in Agile transformations, influencing the direction, adoption, and success of Agile practices within an organization. In Agile methodologies, leaders are not just managers but catalysts for change who guide teams through the complexities of transforming traditional processes into Agile frameworks. Their responsibilities extend beyond simply endorsing Agile practices; they must actively support and embody the Agile principles to foster a culture of collaboration, transparency, and continuous improvement.

One of the primary roles of leaders in Agile transformations is to create a supportive environment that encourages experimentation and learning. This involves empowering teams to make decisions, providing them with the resources they need, and removing impediments that may hinder progress. Leaders must also champion the Agile mindset, which emphasizes adaptability, customer collaboration, and responding to change. By modeling these behaviors, they help to align the organization's culture with Agile values, ensuring that teams are motivated and equipped to embrace new ways of working.

Effective communication is another critical aspect of leadership in Agile environments. Leaders must facilitate open dialogue between teams and stakeholders, ensuring that there is a clear understanding of goals, expectations, and progress. This involves regularly engaging with teams to gather feedback, address concerns, and celebrate successes. Transparent communication helps to build trust and alignment, which are essential for Agile teams to function effectively and deliver value continuously.

Furthermore, leaders in Agile transformations are responsible for fostering a growth mindset across the organization. This includes supporting ongoing training and development opportunities, encouraging cross-functional collaboration, and promoting a culture of experimentation where failures are viewed as learning opportunities rather than setbacks. By prioritizing these elements, leaders can help to sustain momentum and drive long-term success in Agile initiatives.

Training and Coaching: Importance of training and the role of Agile coaches.

Training and coaching are integral to the success of Agile transformations, providing the foundation for teams and individuals to effectively adopt and excel in Agile practices. Training equips team members with the necessary knowledge and skills to understand and implement Agile methodologies, while coaching offers ongoing guidance and support to help teams refine their practices and overcome challenges.

The importance of training in Agile cannot be overstated. Effective training programs help teams grasp Agile principles, frameworks, and tools, ensuring they have a solid understanding of how to apply these concepts in their daily work. This training often includes workshops, courses, and hands-on exercises that cover various aspects of Agile, such as Scrum, Kanban, and Lean methodologies. By investing in comprehensive training, organizations can accelerate the adoption of Agile practices, reduce the learning curve, and increase the likelihood of successful implementation.

Agile coaches play a pivotal role in this process, serving as mentors and facilitators who guide teams through their Agile journey. Unlike traditional trainers, Agile coaches work closely with teams on a continuous basis, providing personalized support and feedback tailored to their specific needs and challenges. Coaches help teams to navigate the complexities of Agile practices, resolve issues, and continuously improve their processes. They also work to foster a culture of collaboration, accountability, and experimentation, which are essential for Agile success.

Moreover, Agile coaches assist in aligning teams with organizational goals and ensuring that Agile practices are consistently applied across different projects and teams. They often collaborate with leadership to drive change management initiatives, address resistance, and promote a shared understanding of Agile values. By providing ongoing support and guidance, Agile coaches help to sustain momentum, build high-performing teams, and ultimately achieve the desired outcomes of Agile transformations. Their role is crucial in bridging the gap between theoretical knowledge and practical application, ensuring that Agile practices are effectively embedded into the organization's culture and operations.

Chapter 9: Future of Agile

Emerging Trends: Latest trends and innovations in Agile.

Agile methodologies continue to evolve, incorporating new trends and innovations that reflect changes in technology, organizational needs, and industry practices. Here are some of the latest trends and innovations shaping the Agile landscape:

1. **Hybrid Agile Models**: Organizations are increasingly adopting hybrid Agile models that combine Agile principles with other methodologies like Waterfall or DevOps. This approach allows teams to leverage the benefits of Agile while addressing the specific needs of projects that require a more structured or sequential approach. Hybrid models can provide greater flexibility and help organizations balance agility with compliance and other requirements.
2. **Agile at Scale**: Scaling Agile practices to large, complex organizations remains a key focus. Frameworks like the Scaled Agile Framework (SAFe), Large Scale Scrum (LeSS), and the Disciplined Agile Delivery (DAD) provide structured approaches to scaling Agile across multiple teams and departments. These frameworks aim to synchronize efforts, improve coordination, and ensure alignment with organizational goals at a larger scale.
3. **Integration of AI and Machine Learning**: The integration of Artificial Intelligence (AI) and Machine Learning (ML) into Agile practices is gaining traction. AI tools are being used to enhance various aspects of Agile, such as automated testing, predictive analytics for project forecasting, and intelligent task management. These technologies can help teams make data-driven decisions, improve efficiency, and reduce manual effort.
4. **Remote and Distributed Agile Teams**: The rise of remote and distributed work has led to innovations in how Agile teams collaborate and communicate. Tools and practices have evolved to support virtual stand-ups, remote retrospectives, and online collaboration. Innovations in digital whiteboarding, video conferencing, and collaboration platforms are helping teams maintain productivity and engagement regardless of their physical location.

5. **Agile Coaching and Transformation Tools**: The role of Agile coaches is expanding with the development of new tools and platforms that support Agile transformation. These tools offer capabilities for tracking progress, assessing team performance, and providing real-time feedback. They also facilitate better coaching and mentoring by offering insights and recommendations based on data analytics.
6. **Focus on Continuous Delivery and DevOps Integration**: Continuous Delivery (CD) and DevOps practices are increasingly being integrated with Agile methodologies to enhance software delivery pipelines. The emphasis on automating deployment processes, continuous integration, and rapid feedback loops helps Agile teams deliver value more frequently and reliably.
7. **Emphasis on Agile Leadership**: There is a growing recognition of the importance of Agile leadership in driving successful transformations. Leaders are being encouraged to adopt Agile principles themselves, support team autonomy, and foster a culture of experimentation and learning. Agile leadership focuses on empowering teams, facilitating collaboration, and guiding organizations through change.
8. **Customer-Centric Agile**: Agile practices are becoming more customer-centric, with a greater emphasis on understanding and addressing customer needs and feedback. Techniques such as Design Thinking are being integrated with Agile to ensure that products and services are aligned with customer expectations and deliver genuine value.

These trends and innovations reflect the dynamic nature of Agile methodologies, highlighting their adaptability and ongoing relevance in a rapidly changing environment. As organizations continue to explore and implement these advancements, Agile practices are likely to evolve further, driving greater efficiency, collaboration, and customer satisfaction.

Agile in Non-Software Environments: Applications of Agile outside software development.

Agile methodologies, originally developed for software development, have found valuable applications in a variety of non-software environments. By focusing on principles like iterative progress, collaboration, and adaptability, Agile can enhance performance and efficiency across different fields. Here are some notable applications of Agile outside of traditional software development:

1. **Marketing**: Agile practices are increasingly used in marketing to improve campaign management and responsiveness. Marketing teams apply Agile principles to manage campaigns in sprints, allowing them to test, iterate, and optimize strategies based on real-time feedback and analytics. This approach helps marketers quickly adapt to market trends, customer preferences, and campaign performance.
2. **Product Management**: Agile is utilized in product management to streamline the development of new products or enhancements. Product managers use Agile techniques to prioritize features, manage backlogs, and conduct regular reviews. This iterative process helps ensure that product development is aligned with customer needs and market demands, leading to more successful product launches.
3. **Human Resources (HR)**: In HR, Agile practices are applied to improve processes such as recruitment, onboarding, and employee engagement. Agile HR teams use iterative cycles to enhance HR initiatives, gather feedback from employees, and make continuous improvements. This approach fosters a more responsive and adaptive HR function that can better meet the needs of the workforce.
4. **Education**: Agile methodologies are being adopted in educational settings to support curriculum development, project-based learning, and instructional design. Educators use Agile principles to create flexible learning environments, iteratively develop lesson plans, and adjust teaching strategies based on student feedback. This iterative approach can enhance student engagement and learning outcomes.
5. **Healthcare**: Agile practices are applied in healthcare to improve patient care processes, administrative functions, and healthcare innovation. Teams use Agile methods to manage projects related to healthcare delivery, process improvement, and technology implementation. This helps in addressing challenges and improving outcomes through iterative testing and feedback.
6. **Manufacturing**: Agile principles are used in manufacturing to enhance product development, supply chain management, and production processes. Agile methodologies support iterative design, rapid prototyping, and continuous improvement, helping manufacturers respond quickly to market changes and customer needs.

7. **Event Planning**: Agile is applied to event planning to manage complex logistics, coordinate multiple teams, and adapt to changes. Event planners use Agile practices to break down tasks into manageable sprints, gather feedback from stakeholders, and make adjustments to ensure successful event execution.
8. **Financial Services**: In financial services, Agile methodologies are used to improve project management, regulatory compliance, and customer service. Agile helps financial institutions to adapt to regulatory changes, manage risk, and enhance customer experiences through iterative improvements and responsive decision-making.

These applications of Agile in non-software environments demonstrate its versatility and effectiveness in fostering collaboration, flexibility, and continuous improvement across various domains. By adapting Agile principles to different contexts, organizations can achieve greater efficiency and responsiveness in their operations.

The Evolution of Agile Practices: How Agile is evolving and adapting to new challenges.

The evolution of Agile practices reflects the methodology's adaptability to new challenges and changing environments. As organizations face increasingly complex and dynamic conditions, Agile has continued to evolve to address these needs, incorporating new practices and frameworks to enhance its effectiveness. Here are some key ways Agile is evolving:

1. **Integration with Other Methodologies**: Agile is increasingly being integrated with other methodologies such as Lean, DevOps, and Design Thinking. This hybrid approach combines Agile's iterative and incremental principles with Lean's focus on reducing waste, DevOps' emphasis on continuous delivery and integration, and Design Thinking's user-centered design. This integration helps organizations address diverse challenges by leveraging the strengths of multiple methodologies.
2. **Scaling Agile Practices**: As organizations grow and projects become more complex, scaling Agile practices has become a major focus. Frameworks like the Scaled Agile Framework (SAFe), Large Scale Scrum (LeSS), and Disciplined Agile Delivery (DAD) have been developed to provide structured approaches for implementing Agile across multiple teams and departments. These

frameworks aim to ensure alignment, coordination, and effective delivery at scale.
3. **Agile in Non-Software Domains**: Agile practices are being applied beyond traditional software development to areas such as marketing, HR, product management, and education. This expansion demonstrates Agile's versatility and ability to improve processes and outcomes in various fields. The adaptation of Agile to different contexts involves modifying practices to fit specific needs while maintaining core principles like iterative progress and collaboration.
4. **Emphasis on Agile Leadership**: The role of leadership in Agile is evolving to focus more on fostering a culture of agility and supporting team autonomy. Agile leaders are increasingly seen as facilitators and coaches rather than traditional managers. They are responsible for guiding teams, removing impediments, and promoting an environment where experimentation and continuous improvement are encouraged.
5. **Adoption of Advanced Technologies**: The integration of advanced technologies such as Artificial Intelligence (AI) and Machine Learning (ML) is influencing Agile practices. AI tools are being used to automate tasks, provide predictive analytics, and enhance decision-making. Agile teams are also exploring how these technologies can support continuous integration, automated testing, and real-time feedback.
6. **Focus on Customer-Centricity**: Agile practices are increasingly centered around customer needs and experiences. Techniques like Agile User Stories, Customer Journey Mapping, and frequent user feedback are being emphasized to ensure that products and services deliver genuine value. This customer-centric approach helps organizations stay aligned with market demands and enhance user satisfaction.
7. **Enhanced Remote Collaboration**: The rise of remote and distributed work has led to innovations in how Agile teams collaborate and communicate. Tools and practices have evolved to support virtual stand-ups, online retrospectives, and digital collaboration. The use of advanced collaboration platforms and virtual whiteboards helps maintain productivity and team cohesion in remote environments.
8. **Greater Focus on Metrics and Data-Driven Decisions**: Agile practices are increasingly incorporating data-driven approaches to measure progress and performance. Agile teams are using metrics and analytics to track key performance indicators (KPIs), assess the impact of changes, and make informed

decisions. This focus on data helps improve transparency and accountability.

The evolution of Agile practices reflects a continuous adaptation to new challenges and opportunities. By integrating with other methodologies, scaling practices, expanding to new domains, and embracing advanced technologies, Agile remains a dynamic and relevant approach for managing complex projects and driving organizational success.

Conclusion

Moving Forward: Guidance on implementing and evolving Agile practices in your organization.

Implementing and evolving Agile practices in an organization requires careful planning, continuous adaptation, and strong leadership. Here's a guide to help you successfully adopt and refine Agile practices within your organization:

1. Start with a Clear Vision

- **Define Objectives**: Clearly articulate why you are adopting Agile and what you hope to achieve. This could include improving project delivery speed, enhancing team collaboration, or increasing customer satisfaction.
- **Identify Key Stakeholders**: Engage leadership, team members, and other stakeholders early on to gain support and align objectives. Their buy-in is crucial for a successful transition.

2. Educate and Train

- **Provide Training**: Offer comprehensive training to teams and leaders on Agile principles, practices, and frameworks. This might include formal workshops, online courses, or hands-on coaching.
- **Focus on Agile Mindset**: Beyond the mechanics of Agile frameworks, emphasize the importance of the Agile mindset—embracing change, iterative progress, and customer collaboration.

3. Choose the Right Framework

- **Select an Appropriate Framework**: Depending on your organization's needs and structure, choose an Agile framework that best fits your context. Scrum, Kanban, or SAFe are popular choices, but you may need a hybrid approach.
- **Pilot Projects**: Start with a few pilot projects to test the chosen framework. This allows for experimentation and adjustment before a full-scale rollout.

4. Foster a Collaborative Culture

- **Promote Open Communication**: Encourage transparent and frequent communication within teams and across the organization. Regular stand-ups, retrospectives, and feedback sessions are essential.
- **Empower Teams**: Allow teams to self-organize and make decisions about their work. Empowerment fosters accountability and innovation.

5. Implement Agile Practices

- **Start Small**: Begin with foundational practices like iterative development, regular reviews, and incremental delivery. Gradually expand as teams become more comfortable with Agile.
- **Use Agile Tools**: Leverage Agile tools and software to manage backlogs, track progress, and facilitate collaboration. Tools like Jira, Trello, or Asana can be useful.

6. Measure and Adapt

- **Track Progress**: Use Agile metrics such as velocity, cycle time, and burn-down charts to monitor progress and identify areas for improvement.
- **Gather Feedback**: Regularly solicit feedback from team members and stakeholders to understand what's working and what needs adjustment.
- **Iterate and Improve**: Continuously refine your Agile practices based on feedback and performance data. Agile is about adapting and evolving, so be prepared to make adjustments as needed.

7. Support and Develop Leaders

- **Agile Leadership**: Equip leaders with the skills to support Agile teams. This includes facilitating collaboration, removing impediments, and fostering a culture of continuous improvement.
- **Coaching**: Consider bringing in Agile coaches to guide teams through challenges and provide personalized support.

8. Scale and Integrate

- **Scaling Agile**: As Agile practices mature, consider scaling them across the organization using frameworks like SAFe or LeSS if necessary.

- **Integrate with Other Practices**: Combine Agile with other methodologies or practices like Lean, DevOps, or Design Thinking to address broader organizational needs and improve overall effectiveness.

9. Foster Continuous Learning

- **Encourage Experimentation**: Promote a culture where teams feel safe to experiment and learn from failures. This can lead to innovation and continuous improvement.
- **Invest in Ongoing Training**: Keep teams updated with the latest Agile practices and trends through continuous learning opportunities.

10. Communicate Successes and Challenges

- **Share Success Stories**: Highlight successful Agile projects and outcomes to reinforce the value of Agile practices and inspire others.
- **Address Challenges Openly**: Acknowledge and address challenges transparently. This builds trust and helps the organization collectively work towards solutions.

By following these steps, organizations can effectively implement Agile practices and continuously evolve them to meet changing needs and challenges. The key is to maintain a flexible and adaptive approach, focusing on collaboration, continuous improvement, and delivering value.